HOW TO ACHIEVE
TOTAL SUCCESS

How to Use the Power of Creative Thought

by

RUSS VON HOELSCHER

PUBLISHED BY
George Sterne
Profit Ideas
254 E. Grand Avenue
Escondido, CA 92025

First edition   1983
First printing   1983
Second printing   1984
Third printing   1984
Fourth printing   1985
Fifth printing   1986

First soft cover edition   1987
Second soft cover edition   1988
Third soft cover edition   1990

PROFIT IDEAS
254 E. Grand Avenue
Escondido, CA 92025

ISBN: 0-940398-19-2

HOW TO ACHIEVE TOTAL SUCCESS

TABLE OF CONTENTS

ACKNOWLEDGEMENTS

I am pleased to gratefully acknowledge some of those who aided me in the labor of making this book, *How to Achieve Total Success*, a reality.

I wish to lovingly thank Anna Westmoreland for her love and support on a daily basis; George Sterne for publishing this work; Mim Luikart for typing the manuscript; Linda Lantz for the indexing; and Alexia Conrad for the cover and dust jacket design.

Special thanks to Ken Keyes, Jr., for his words of wisdom that have been added to my manuscript and help to make this an important book. I highly recommend all of Ken's wonderful conscious-raising books and his seminars and workshops.

"WORDS ARE THE
MOST CREATIVE FORCE
IN THE UNIVERSE."

Foreword

Why are you interested in a book entitled *How to Achieve Total Success*? Most likely it is because in some areas of your life (finances, health, relationships, self-esteem, etc.,) you see room for improvement. This is true of most of us. But what this book is about is more than that. The Total Success philosophy and guidelines presented here are timeless. Although this work may be judged philosophical in nature, it is also very pragmatic. It is not just another interesting "how-to-do-it" book. It is a book about using your most valuable asset—*your mind*—to achieve success in all areas of living. The same "right thinking" that can make your relationships work will also work to help you reach your financial goals. The same positive thinking that will keep you healthy can make you happy. In short, this book is here to tell you: YES! You can have it all!

On the path to Total Success, you must first be completely willing to divorce yourself from undesirable thoughts and patterns of the past. This is not an easy task, but it is an essential one. Too often, the way one becomes unknowingly conditioned to think is the built-in major barrier to achieving true success. A fatalistic tendency to accept certain conditions as inevitable, "the way life is," presents a success roadblock that must be removed. As Julius Caesar reflected, "The fault, dear Brutus, lies not in our stars, but in ourselves . . . "

Secondly, you must expand your viewpoint. This means developing an eagerness to encounter new ideas, studying them and assimilating those which best serve your personal success requirements and success goals.

The third important factor necessary to obtaining true success is your ability to define, set and achieve goals. Nothing is more instrumental in helping men and women achieve success. Defining, setting and achieving goals is the pathway to abundant living. The paramount thing to remember about goals is this: with goals, nearly everything is possible; without goals, almost nothing is. Goals separate life's winners from the losers.

Winners are people who relate successfully to themselves and others. Losers do not! You were born a winner, and this book will show you how to recognize and effectively use the valuable hidden assets you already possess.

This is not a religious book; it is not a theoretical guide; nor is it a psychology textbook. It is not meant as a substitute for psychiatric treatment or a do-it-yourself psychoanalysis home kit. This is a practical book that will present proven formulas and ageless wisdom that can enable you to obtain success in all areas of your life.

Knowledge alone, however, will not bring smashing success to you. You must bring true desire to this study and be totally willing to put the life-changing principles presented here into action. Above, below, within and beyond everything else, you must be willing to learn to love everyone unconditionally, including yourself. *Love is the answer and the ultimate power!*

The totally successful person is rich in love, faith, self-esteem, health, friendships and personalized achievements, as well as being financially independent. Wealth is very important in today's society, but to seek financial freedom alone is not enough. Presented here is a total personal program on how you can achieve "Total Success," and thus, total freedom. *When you are totally successful and totally free, YOU HAVE GOT IT ALL!*

"You can't really cope with your existence till you're a whole person . . . "

— **FRITZ PERLS**

Chapter One

WHAT'S WRONG WITH ME?

"What is wrong with me? Why am I like this?" We've all asked ourselves this question at one time or another.

Behind this perplexing question lies the root question: Is it possible for someone with my background, my education, my personality, my family history, my age and my skills to obtain success? The answer to this question is a definite **"YES!"**

If you are willing to change your mind and cultivate a new MENTAL OUTLOOK, you can overcome your fears, inhibitions, low self-esteem and all other roadblocks to success. The way you think about yourself and your condition affects all decisions you make. To change your mind is to change your life. To learn how to think is to learn how to live.

At the core of our uncertainty and low self-esteem are our mental blocks, confusions, misconceptions, prejudices and insecurities. Therein lies our problem, but here is the good news: You can change your outlook on life! You can develop healthy self-esteem, optimism, trust, joy and confidence. You can change your outlook because you are its creator. It's *your* mind! By choosing your thoughts wisely, your outlook can change and your life can be new, exciting and rewarding. By learning to love yourself unconditionally, you can learn to love others and love life!

To gain control over your mind is to gain control of your

life. If this book does nothing more than motivate you to consciously choose your thoughts and reactions, it will have had a positive, life-changing effect on you.

Chances are good that you are very selective about the kinds of people you allow into your home. You would not want thieves, troublemakers and destructive individuals visiting you. You have every right to be selective in choosing your friends and associates. You should also be extremely selective about the thoughts you permit to enter your mind. Thoughts associated with fear and frustrations, jealousies and hate, lack and limitations ultimately can do you a greater injustice than a common thief who would steal material goods.

FEAR: MENTAL ENEMY NO. 1

Although human problems come in all sizes, shapes, colors and categories, at the bottom line of most of our problems is that ugly four-letter word: FEAR. Fear is the mind's worst enemy and it raises extreme havoc when we allow it to enter and dominate our thoughts. Once allowed to enter, fear will always fight for control and total mental domination. That is the nature of this insidious enemy.

While fear can come to us in any of hundreds of different forms, there appear to be eight major fears that humans allow themselves to suffer most from. Please don't become uneasy if you recognize several of your pet fears here. Almost everyone suffers from a combination of these demonic little jewels from time to time. The key factor lies in degrees.

The eight major fears:
1. the fear of going crazy
2. the fear of failure
3. the fear of sickness
4. the fear of poverty
5. the fear of not being loved
6. the fear of loss of love
7. the fear of old age
8. the fear of death

All other fears are insignificant compared to these eight and can be categorized within the above eight headings.

Now, let's take a penetrating look at these fearful goblins and shine some light on them.

THE FEAR OF GOING CRAZY

The fear of being crazy or going there is one of the most prevalent fears people have, yet is seldom talked about. While it could be said with some justification that most of us are a little crazy or neurotic, at least some of the time, only a small percent of the population is medically and/or legally judged to be mentally ill, psychotic or insane.

Most fear is 100% negative; however, some degree of PROTECTIVE FEAR (awareness is a better word) can be positive in protecting us against accidents, pitfalls, etc., and this also applies to the fear of going crazy or of being crazy.

First of all, no one fearful of going crazy *is* crazy. The seriously mentally ill seldom see themselves in their true condition. Fear of craziness is not craziness itself.

What is behind the fear of going crazy? Generally, psychologists have found that such thoughts are not at all directly related to what is really "crazy" or neurotic in a person. Almost every person has wide-ranging and different concepts of what crazy is and what is crazy about them. In many cases this fear is related to a great deal of anxiety brought up by confrontation with hitherto unheard from and unfamiliar desires, impulses and thoughts.

Feelings that one has never experienced before can cause one to doubt his or her mental balance. This condition is common among teenagers, the newly married (or anyone involved in a serious relationship for the first time), those who lose someone through death or divorce, loss of a steady job or any other "interruptions" in our living patterns. At the root of the fear of craziness is some form of intense stress caused by change which seems to threaten our very existence. Fear can only exist in an atmosphere where love is vacant or in short supply.

Below is a social-readjusting rate scale developed by Doctors Thomas H. Holmes and Richard H. Rahe which attempts to measure stress in terms of "life events." You will notice stress can be caused by events that could be judged "positive" as well as "negative". People who face several stressful situations are more likely to become physically ill than those who do not. Also, the more stress a person contends with, the more likely the person will be concerned with fears of physical or mental illness. Listed here are Drs. Holmes and Rahe's 43 most prominent stress-related events.

RANK	EVENT
1	Death of spouse
2	Divorce
3	Marital separation
4	Jail term
5	Death of close family member
6	Personal injury or illness
7	Marriage
8	Fired from work
9	Marital reconciliation
10	Retirement
11	Change in family member's health
12	Pregnancy
13	Sex difficulties
14	Addition to family
15	Business readjustment
16	Change in financial status
17	Death of a close friend
18	Change to a different line of work
19	Change in number of marital arguments
20	Mortgage or loan over $10,000
21	Foreclosure of mortgage or loan
22	Change in work responsibilities
23	Son or daughter leaving home
24	Trouble with in-laws
25	Outstanding personal achievement
26	Spouse begins or stops work
27	Starting or finishing school
28	Change in living conditions
29	Revision of personal habits
30	Trouble with boss
31	Change in work hours, conditions
32	Change in residence
33	Change in schools
34	Change in recreational habits
35	Change in church activities
36	Change in social activities
38	Change in sleeping habits

39 Change in number of family gatherings
40 Change in eating habits
41 Vacation
42 Christmas season
43 Minor violation of the law

Many believe fear causes stress; others think stress causes our fears. One thing is certain: the removal of either one will help dissipate the other.

Fear of mental illness is not craziness. Serious mental illness is more related to establishing greater distance between one's self and the rest of the world. It involves massive distortions in perceived reality, which manifests delusions and hallucinations. Thankfully only a small percentage of humans reach this condition.

You and I may be slightly "bonkers", but the odds against reaching a legal and medical definition of insanity are very remote. If thoughts of craziness persist over long periods of time, psychiatric help may be advisable. Millions of people the world over are seeing competent psychiatrists, psychologists, family therapists and other mental health professionals. Taking action to correct a problem is anything but crazy. It is the most sane thing a person can do.

THE FEAR OF FAILURE

The fear of failure and the fear of criticism are closely related. This fear is a major stumbling stone in the path toward success and self-actualization.

Isn't it incredible that our fear of lack of success can

actually rob us of the opportunity to be successful? Yet, this is a fact.

The Willingness to Fail

The time, energy and devotion many people spend in making their failure a reality could bring them SMASHING SUCCESSES.

Although thousands of positive thinking, self-help and metaphysical books have been written and read by millions, the majority of people continue their love affair with failure. The same thrust of personal energy needed to bring success is required to fail. It takes energy to fail. Failure is misspent energy poured into the wrong bottomless pit. This appears to be a paradox, but it isn't. It is absolute truth, although difficult to understand at first.

Success and failure seem to be, but are not, exact opposites. We may see success as awareness, alertness, that which is active and alive; thus, we may share the common attitude of failure as being inactive, lethargic and suffering from inertia. While there is some truth in these definitions, it does not convey that no energy is being spent. An enormous amount of energy must be used to resist forward motion. A colossal struggle must be fought against man's natural forces of life, success, discovery and movement in order to remain inert. Although this battle may be waged far below the surface, it requires much energy. The person who sits immobile, staring at housework and cleaning that needs tending to or resists the heap of business and/or personal mail on their desk, may refuse physical action to correct these situations. However, the energy spent to resist these necessary duties will

17

render them just as physically and mentally tired at the end of the day or even more so than if they dug in and got the job done. The procrastinator pays the price for his lack of action.

The Rewards of Failure

Failure is not without some compensation. The man or woman who fails through wrong action or through procrastination will be spared some anxiety associated with the risks one must be willing to take in hopes of succeeding. Also, failure by not taking action will not be blatantly visible to others who might see an attempt at success missing the mark. Nevertheless, quiet failure will always be apparent to the person who fails. Failure is never easy to live with and is never comfortable.

The willingness to fail is misguided thinking personified. The same MIND POWER that can be channeled to propel us to success can allow us to fail by inactivity or by wrong thinking and misguided activity.

Although our natural nature drives us toward success in all areas of living, we can self-teach ourselves or let others teach us the art of failure. Here are just some of the ways we may sabotage our own good: Lack of self-esteem *(you must believe in yourself totally to be successful)*; lack of true desire *(success only comes to those who really want it)*; procrastination *(inactivity is one of the most common ways to fail by default)*; excessive use of alcohol or drugs *(these two vices are enemies of those who would win success and also thieves, who can steal victory from people who already have achieved success)*; too much sleep *(recent studies indi-*

18

cate most Americans oversleep two to three hours per night, thus wasting away up to eighty productive hours in a single month); the lack of concrete goals (*it is possible to be active and "work for success" only to fail miserably because one has not defined his goals. Without goals, how can you know you have arrived?*).

While there are many other possible explanations for failure, the above methods are among the worst culprits.

Knowing that you can program yourself to fail, just as you can program yourself for success, and that both offer a payoff, you must realize the rewards of success are immeasurably more satisfying. There can be the rich objective rewards of achieving financial independence. Also, there is no way to measure the immense joy one experiences in knowing he or she has reached a significant goal. Victory is always sweet to the believers and achievers.

The world may not criticize a failure, although it often does, but the failure never stops criticizing himself, especially when he becomes aware that the same amount of effort, properly channeled, could have brought success.

The world will often criticize a successful person. That is to say, while many will congratulate and praise your success, several others will put you down. Not everyone likes a successful person. Failures, in particular, tend to resent the successful. That is just another reason why they are unsuccessful. The approval of others is a poor motivator in itself. The joy you feel from within, knowing you have given your best, is sheer ecstasy and is the priceless gift to all who demand the best that they can give. Success is not just the feeling you get when you reach your goal. It is also the great feelings you experience as you strive for your goals.

Don't worship at the altar of approval

Closely related to our fear of criticism is the human obsession to receive constant approval. While it is quite natural to enjoy the praise and admiration of others as a result of our achievements and positive personality traits, an over-developed reliance on the approval of others is not a productive asset.

Other people are not the source of your good, *and* we need people in our lives. In fact, people can be the channel through which prosperity, love and happiness flow, but they are not the source of the good you desire. God is your source. Regardless of how you relate to God: in the conventional Judeo-Christian belief; in the metaphysical sense; a combination of these two, or simply as life itself or the life within you. This is your source.

When we believe other people are the source of our love, abundance, security, happiness, etc., we make them into our gods. By turning to our mates, parents, children, friends, employers, even the government, in hopes of filling our cup with health, wealth, happiness and security, we are in danger of losing our precious gift of self-reliance.

By believing that our good must come from others, we fall into the trap of becoming dependent on their approval. Once the need to be approved (acknowledged, loved and/or liked by others) gets out of hand, it can have the same emotional effect on people as cocaine has on the physical level. It can rob us of our self-esteem and reduce us to a state of hapless dependency, emotional Jello.

Please don't misunderstand what I am saying here. We need to give and receive love. There is nothing wrong with getting deserved recognition from others. Self-reliance in no way denotes separation from other human beings. We simply must not become a slave to our egos. If we do, our mental/emotional nature goes on "tilt", and we surrender our power to others. When we worship at the altar of approval, we make other people our gods—an overwhelming responsibility they are not suited to fulfill. While they may fulfill our demanding emotional needs for a time, eventually they will likely disappoint us. This brings with it more emotional pain, uncertainty, even feelings of betrayal and rejection.

Go to your source for your good. Let other people be positive channels of your good, and equals with whom you share the fun, love and excitement which is life.

THE FEAR OF POVERTY

Your mind is capable of bringing you wealth or poverty. Fear of poverty and poverty itself are the result of impoverished mental attitudes. The fear of poverty can be just as destructive as the state of poverty, for if left unchecked, it can reduce one to poverty or keep one in that state of lack and limitation—a never-ceasing struggle just to make ends meet—which is a sorry state of existence.

Associated with poverty is suffering, humility and a feeling of despair. Only those who have experienced poverty understand the full meaning of the condition. However, most of us

21

have experienced a degree of poverty, even if we have never been bankrupt or flat broke. The fear of poverty is another matter. While it may not render us busted or completely broken, it certainly can prevent us from reaching success. This fear brings self-doubt, distorts reason, destroys creative imagination, robs us of our self-reliance, dulls enthusiasm and replaces desire with despair. If allowed to grow and fester, it can kill our initiative and success-drive, and leave us in a mire of uncertainty, doubt, procrastination and a feeling of powerlessness.

The seven symptoms of poverty fear

1. low self-esteem
2. lack of motivation
3. indecision
4. doubt
5. worry
6. lack of faith
7. procrastination

Low self-esteem

At the head of this list is low self-esteem, and frankly, all other symptoms could be summed up under this impoverished condition. Low self-esteem means little or no self-love. When we are not expressing healthy, vibrant self-love, it is impossible to love and respect others or to love life itself. While no one is attractive very long to a person expressing egocentric self-love, people in harmony with themselves in spirit, mind and body are always radiating positive self-love. These are the people we love to be near!

Lack of motivation is prevalent where ambition is missing. People who embrace mental and physical laziness may not sink to the depths of poverty, although they could. Often they are able to "just get by," viewing their life and their jobs as a never-ending struggle, which in fact is exactly what they have become.

Indecision is particularly dangerous. When you refuse to take a stand and make decisions, someone else usually will come along to make your decisions for you. The result is usually anything but self-satisfying.

Doubt is very closely related to low self-esteem. It often invades the consciousness of those who have tried once or twice and missed the mark. Instead of jumping back in the race, as a winner must, they become fearful of taking a new risk and often criticize those who do.

Worry is common among those who are mistake-prone. Some people program their minds for success; others program failure. The failure-types are stuck in a rut, victims of their own endless treadmill. If this condition is not eradicated, these folks often slip into depression, frown constantly and neglect personal appearances. Excessive drinking, compulsive overeating and even the use of narcotics are a danger if the person consumed with worry also has a compulsive nature.

Lack of faith breeds negativity. *The winners in life are all believers.* Those lacking in faith are beaten before they begin. Nothing great was ever accomplished by over-cautious types who had no faith. Anyone can find the negative side in every situation. America would never have been discovered if someone with faith had not taken a chance. The car you drive, the airplane you fly in and the television you spend too much time watching were once considered "impossible" ideas by those who could not dream nor dared to express faith.

Procrastination stops success cold. It is an absolute destructive state of mind and being. The procrastinator may think he is conserving energy, but actually he is spending it in large degrees without reaping any of its benefits. This symptom is a cousin of lack of faith. The procrastinator shirks responsibility due to self-doubt. It is always associated with people deep in a rut who don't know, and who look for, an excuse not to try. It is the symptom of the beaten who, by doing nothing, accept their defeats. It renders people immobile and at the mercy of anyone who would take decisive action.

In summing up, the fear of poverty is the chief villain that interferes with thoughts of abundance and the "can do" attitude. While few of us express perfection and are without some occasional self-doubt, we must consciously drive the fear of poverty from our minds or it can deliver that state which we dread. Think positively and act abundantly and watch the fear of poverty flee!

THE FEAR OF NOT BEING LOVED

The fear of not being loved is another common, yet insidious, state of mind. It is closely related to our need for approval, but it is an even stronger concern. Untold miseries are wrought by those who believe they are unloved.

We can say, without qualification, "love approval" preoccupies a great many of our waking hours and can be our foremost concern. We really can't allow ourselves to fear being unloved. Not if happiness is our goal.

The natural spirit of each person is a joyous combination of freedom and love. The only meaningful relationships are those founded on love, freedom, support, openness and unpossessiveness. And yet many of our relationships are anything but free, loving, supportive, open or unpossessive. We cry out that freedom is a high, desirable virtue, yet we are too often ready to accept, even demand, unnecessary restrictions. In our close relationships (mates, children, parents), what could be a loving union becomes an interdependent tangle of unfulfilled emotions, anxiety, stress and self-imposed and self-inflicted bondage. Our thoughts about love can easily become confused with our feelings on the subject. We often accept something that isn't true love at all. Love feelings may become mixed with uncontrolled thoughts and feelings of jealousy, guilt, domination and control. The only thing we are certain of is that we are experiencing something very strong that has us emotionally aroused. Even if this love feeling is not positive, constructive and completely fulfilling, we may desire to grasp it and hold it to our bosom. Like the popular song of recent vintage says, "A little bit of love is better than no love; even a bad love is better than no love . . . . " But is it really? Are we wise to cling to less than the real thing? Is there such a thing as true love?

The answers to those big questions are a qualified "no" to the first and an emphatic "yes" to the second!

The person feeling unloved will do almost anything to get some love. A "little bit of love" may give us some temporary strokes, but it will only whet our appetites for more. Acceptance of all the love another is capable of giving is rational and desirable. Allowing ourselves to express only a small measure of love, while "saving" most of our love, lest we be put in a vulnerable position, just isn't where happiness is at. Many say they are afraid to express their true feelings and their deep love because they were HURT BY LOVE in the past. Not true! Love never hurt anyone. We may have been hurt in the past by a lack of love or by a former lover, but never by love itself. Love always helps, and it always feels good.

When we think love has been painful, in reality we are judging objects of our love (parents, children, mates, etc.), whose response to our feelings about love didn't shape up with our expectations. Real love is not given in order to earn rewards or concessions. The great gift is the giving and not in any expected payoff.

Not that there is anything wrong in both giving and receiving love. This situation is ideal and most desirable in all intimate relationships. One may not choose to remain in an intimate relationships where he or she is not receiving love. However, this should not be reason enough to withhold our love. Love is not meant to be bartered or passed along with conditions attached. If it is true, it is whole and complete and the total gift. Your love for someone is your ultimate personal expression. What is returned to you by them is their expression.

The fear of not being loved stems from a very low self-esteem—a lack of self-love. Grave self-doubts about ourselves can make us feel unloved and unlovable. Although this con dition is totally false (every human being is a child of God, a unique creation who is lovable and deserving of love), it will persist until, by loving himself, the person elevates his self-esteem. A person with a well-developed positive self-image knows that love, happiness and all sorts of other "good stuff" is his birthright.

THE FEAR OF LOSING LOVE

The fear of losing love is based on feelings that we are going to have love taken away from us. We may sense a lover will desert us, a spouse will divorce us, our children will soon leave home, friends will move away or in some way abandon us. This fear stems from a belief that we are going to become losers. Something of precious value may be leaving us. Our first fearful thought usually is: clutch and hold on!

As fears of losing love preoccupy our thoughts, the love experience itself (if, in fact, love was ever present) suffers. Like many fears, the fear itself can help create the undesirable condition.

A tendency to possess or suppress surrounds most of our intimate relationships. If both persons are open, self-confident and committed to enjoying a healthy relationship, all such tendencies are held in check.

Suppression is always motivated by lack—the fear of losing the other person. This fear of losing another manifests itself in a compelling desire to control and possess. In trying to rob another of his free will and power, you actually surrender your own. When you attempt to control another human being, you become very dependent upon that individual for your love, happiness and expression. When you have given away your power to another, sooner or later he will disappoint you and the effect will be crushing!

The way to enjoy love is to free it. Our fear, of course, tells us to hang on tightly. We refuse to release loved ones because we fear we will lose them and their love, erroneously thinking that they will love us for strangling them emotionally. As the suppression and possession process continues, unhappiness increases. The relationship usually begins to fall apart. Communication becomes guarded or nonexistent. We don't say what we mean, and we don't mean what we say. We don't act or live the way we really want to. We may become dishonest and secretive because we fear honesty and openness will help destroy the already deteriorating relationship. Naturally, the opposite is true. Honesty, openness and love given for its own beautiful sake are the only way to save and enhance the relationship. Developing a healthy sense of self-love is how to overcome fears of ever losing love. You can't lose what you yourself are!

THE FEAR OF ILLNESS

At first, one would suspect that the fear of physical illness could be put in the same category with fear of mental illness. The person fearing one probably would be fearful of the other, right? Wrong! While some people experience both fears, most choose to be fearful of one and not the other. Although many "choose" mental problems to be fearful of, even more people are concerned with potential physical ailments.

While it is prudent to be concerned with our health, the fear of illness, like most fears, is not beneficial. It is a big stress-builder and insidious enemy of one's peace of mind.

The fear of illness is closely associated with fears of aging and death. However, we are going to comment on them individually since all three have several singular aspects. People fear ill health because they fear restriction of their ability to express more life-living. They also fear the financial burden associated with sickness.

Hypochondria (imagined sickness) runs rampant in today's society. Over 50% of all people visiting physicians for professional service suffer from hypochondria. And their suffering is real, for if the mind is misled into believing illness is present, the symptoms and displeasures are no less evident and intense than if "real illness" were present.

When we realize that health is our natural God-ordained state of being and that healthy thoughts are the best medicine for our physical bodies, we will understand the truth about disease. The word disease literally means not to be at ease— the opposite of being at peace with oneself. Thus, the fear of disease is indicative of disease condition within the mind.

As the medical profession increasingly tends to view human health as a holistic system, the relationship between mind, emotions and body can be seen as interrelated and three parts of a coequal unit.

When one realizes the powerful influence the mind has on our emotions and physical bodies, it is not difficult to understand that the fear of ill health, even disease itself, can be greatly influenced by the thoughts contained in both our conscious and subconscious mind. The fear of disease and the physical condition of disease result from an imbalance in a person's mental-emotional-physical makeup. When you are overly concerned with your health, your mind can become filled with thoughts of potential problems. This stirs up your emotions, and the physical result can be a great degree of stress. Even if the illness is "imaginary", the mental, emotional and physical stress is in itself an unhealthful condition.

When one views Mind as a first cause, it is not difficult to understand the concept *YOUR MIND CAN KEEP YOU WELL.*

THE FEAR OF OLD AGE

While many fears can be said to be totally unfounded in regard to reality, the fear of old age can be laid to the fact that we are all getting older. An eleven-year-old girl recently lamented on her age: "I used to love to play with my dolls, but that was before I got to be so old." The fact that we are getting older can lead to negative thoughts such as: I can't have fun any more; I can't do some of the things I used to like doing; my looks are diminishing and/or my personal value is decreasing. Let's look at this fear up close.

Here are seven basic reasons why many people (perhaps most of us) fear aging:

1. Increased susceptibility to injury and ailments
2. Loss of beauty (youthful appearance, etc.)
3. Erosion of physical strength
4. Pronounced prejudices many people have against older people
5. The need to depend more on others
6. The loss of some people we love
7. The approach of death

No one is immune to sickness, injury or nagging ailments because of his age. While it is true that a young man of twenty-one is less likely to be injured in strenuous activities than an older man of seventy-one, the senior citizen should know far more about his tolerance level, body needs and physical limitations.

It's true—senior citizens usually do not engage in the very same activities (although there are marvelous exceptions to this rule) as do their youthful counterparts. But then, doesn't each stage of life (childhood, youth, early adulthood, etc.) bring with it interest in new pursuits and activities? A reluctance to give up the things of the past can keep us *stuck* in the past.

As to the belief that age robs us of our beauty (good looks), that thought is highly subjective. Physical strength may decrease somewhat even if the older person eats well and exercises regularly, but in most cases, great strength is not required by the senior. Developed skills are far more important today than enormous physical strength.

I will not make a foolish statement by telling anyone that there are no prejudices with regard to the aging. There are. Many young and middle-aged people are very unkind in thought and deed concerning seniors. Even worse, many seniors are contemptuous in their treatment of each other. This is unexcusable behavior. However, as pointed out by Reverend Terry Cole-Whittaker in her book, *What You Think of Me is None of My Business,* **"we all have enough of a challenge to clear our own minds concerning our negative thoughts without worrying about what others might say or think."**

The need to depend more on others (family, friends or those in the helping professions) is another aging fear that is a fact of life for some and someday will be for others. However, many folks remain self-reliant all their lives, and if you should ever need help from others, remember that the reward of service goes to both the giver and receiver. Many times the individual fearing he will need help from others is the same person who has never gone out of his way to lend a hand. *As you sow, so shall you reap,* the Bible wisely reminds us.

As one goes through life, people and conditions do change. Former lovers and/or mates leave, children grow up and establish their own lives, friends may move and death is a reality. Still, the person who has a healthy amount of self-love and who sends love to others will always be surrounded with love.

THE FEAR OF DEATH

The fear of death is very strong no matter what your age bracket is. While death, like taxes, may be inevitable, thoughts of life and love can actually keep us fit, alive and happy much longer.

For those who believe in life after life, death is cheated of any final victory. Think about joy, and love and life will take on a dramatic new meaning. The fear of death, like all other kinds of fears is actually what can keep us from free expression and productive living.

Now that we have asked the question, "What's Wrong With Me?" and presented some insights into why we may think we are not okay, it is time to focus on the solutions to our problems/challenges.

Some examples of Total Success principles have been briefly discussed. Now we are going to dig into the fascinating subject of how to make your life more exciting, more healthy, more rewarding, more abundant and happy, and above all: more loving.

What's wrong with you? Not a single thing that some New Thoughts will not correct!

*"To learn how to think
is to learn how to live . . . "*

—ERNEST HOLMES

Chapter Two

Thoughts Come First

Mind is where everything begins. The car you drive to work, the airplane you fly to vacations or business appointments, and the toothbrush you routinely use each morning are simply the physical manifestation of someone's creative thought. And so it is with *everything*. Someone wise once said: *"From nothing (thoughts) comes everything!"*

The greatest discovery man has ever made or can make is the realization that thought is cause, and everything we see, touch or experience is the effect of creative thinking. If we can think, we already have the ability to create. The power to create is intrinsically present in anyone who has the ability to think. Knowing this, we need not be concerned with adding creativity to our thinking but rather in developing the techniques required to bring it out. There is nothing new to create. Creation rather waits for our discovery of it. The basic ingredients and resources needed to build a transcontinental jet were available a thousand years ago. People in the eleventh century simply were not mentally tuned in to such things. The technology wasn't present to build a "horseless carriage," much less an airplane, because man's mind was not focused on such a task ten centuries ago.

Everything that is appears to come from nothing—nothing in the sense that it is no-thing! However, a closer examination of thought clearly reveals *thoughts are things*—very real "things" and very powerful things at that. Our thoughts of creating success in any worthwhile endeavor, combined with definite goals, desire, belief and persistence, are the catalyst that make success for us a reality.

YOUR SPIRITUAL NATURE

Metaphysicians, many behavorial psychologists and other truth-seekers give this three-fold definition of man: A "human being" is a spiritual being—a spiritual being that uses a mind and has a body. Spiritual + mental + physical.

It does not matter if you are a religious person or not, as we all can identify with our spiritual (abstract) nature in one way or another. Even the most vocal atheists do not deny life's abstract nature, even though they reject the concept of God.

Electricity is a scientific fact of life. Man knows how to control and use this energy source; yet, no one has ever seen it. Electricity is without color, shape or form. It's real and it works, and yet it is not visible. The spiritual nature of a person is somewhat like electricity—it is a real power, although unseen, and can be controlled and put to very beneficial use in our lives. First we must become aware of this great power, and then we must find the ways and means of giving it direction to bring us the tangible results we desire.

IDEAS MANIFESTED

This world, and everything in it, is the net result of ideas manifested. The mighty oak tree is no more than the lingering evidence of one tiny seed with an "inbred idea" of what it could be. Because ideas put into action create our reality, we are the directors of events and conditions that take place in our experience. Unlike the little kernel that one day will be a huge tree, our fates are not predestined.

Environment and conditions can have profound effects on our lives, but new thinking and new ideas can help transcend all other influences. We are in a sense co-creators. We did not create the whole world, but we co-create the circumstances and conditions of our lives. Our ideas do manifest themselves. What we're experiencing in life (whether we judge it to be good or bad) is related to our present and past thinking patterns. Since our minds are not set in concrete (although at times it may seem so), we can change our circumstances and conditions by merely changing our minds.

YOU ARE THE WRITER, ACTOR, PRODUCER, AND DIRECTOR. IS YOUR PLAY A HIT?

In movies and theatrical plays, someone prepares a script (the author, screenwriter or playwright), others play the roles (the actors) while still others produce and direct the production. Seldom are these duties interchangeable. On the expanded stage that is life, you get to write the script, do the acting under your own self-direction and package and produce the entire show. If you're not getting rave reviews (especially from your chief critic—yourself), it is time for some rewriting, perhaps even a whole new life script, a new leading man or leading lady and stronger self-direction. This can assure a smashing performance, rave reviews from others, and most important of all, great self-satisfaction.

MIND AND BRAIN

The study of thinking and the Science of Thought is a study of Cause, Spirit, Mind and ultimately Universal Intelligence and how universal success principles can be incorporated into individual thinking. While some scientists still contend the brain is the center of all thought, an increasing number of the men and women of science have come to see the brain of man in much the same context as we view a computer—a magnificent computer, but still one that is programed by a higher thinking intelligence. This concept, of course, would be shared by those who study and practice Metaphysics. It is also a viewpoint compatible with many psychological, religious or spiritual beliefs.

There can be no doubt that the human brain is an awesome and magnificent mechanism. Man's high technology has created electronic brains, computers and calculating machines which run smoothly and are wonders of science. But no mechanical brain can duplicate the conscious and subconscious marvels of the human biocomputer. And yet, there is no indication the brain itself is the highest form of intellect or is in control of the mind. More and more thinkers see the mind as using a brain, rather than visa-versa. If one can comprehend the concept that we have a mind that uses a brain, it is often much easier to grasp the principle that we must take dominion over our thoughts and program or re-program ourselves in order to win the success we desire.

SUCCESS STARTS WITH AWARENESS

Within the wonderful word "aware" there is the word ARE. If you want to be successful in all your activities, it is vital that you gain self-realization. Knowing who you really are is the doorway to self-actualization. To be the kind of person you wish to be and to have all that you want to experience, cultivate your awareness. Start by focusing on the here and now. Don't allow your thoughts to ramble. Most unsuccessful people are stuck somewhere in the past or preoccupied by what the future may hold. By realizing that the past is behind us and that the future is only a promise, we can put our energy on what is important here and now. Grasping the significance of the truth that "we only can live in the now" can uproot unproductive thinking and help us take immediate positive action to materialize today's positive thinking.

It is not unwise to learn from the past and make some preparation for the future. Just don't overdo it! What is vitally important is what we do today—right here and right now! Try as we may (and millions are still trying), it is impossible to change the past. Then too, what we think happened in the past and what really did happen often are not one and the same. The past is just that—the past. The future, of course, never quite makes it. By the time it arrives it is always the present. We are forced to live in the here and now. However, we may rebel against this reality and escape to thoughts of past events, usually seeing them in a negative light, or turn our attention to what will happen in the future. The successful person soon stops this exercise in futility and learns the wisdom in the statement: *BE HERE NOW!*

LIFE IS CONSCIOUSNESS

To be alive is the only reality. Life is consciousness and consciousness is all there is. Each human being is an individualized but not separate expression of the all-encompassing Universal Consciousness. Your mind is both conscious and creative, for the two always work together. When our finite minds catch a brief flash of this cosmic reality, it becomes easier to understand why "we are masters of our own destiny."

To have the power of creativity is to hold the golden key that can unlock any door and remove any obstacle. No limit can be placed upon the spirit of man that he cannot remove through conscious application of his creative nature. Metaphysics is a study of Mind, Creativity, First Cause and ultimately Universal Spirit or God. Some people are comfortable contemplating Universal Spirit or God, and others are not. If you have trouble with any of the terms, simply change them. If you relate better to the term First Clause than the term God, use it. However, any discussion on how to use Creative Mind Power to bring success to you is closely related to applied metaphysics.

METAPHYSICS—THE DIVINE SCIENCE

The study of Universal Intelligence or Creative Consciousness is not different from the study of chemistry and physics. Metaphysics starts where physics leaves off. A learned physicist once stated that he perceived the Universe as "an Infinite Thinker, thinking mathematically."

There are many concepts of God. Many religions have personalized God as the all-powerful "Supreme Being." If this is your belief, you can use prayer and meditation to make conscious contact with your personal Creator to seek His guidance in all your affairs. If you, on the other hand, believe in the Universal Oneness of all life and see God as the One Life, One Energy and One Creative Principle (rather than person) in which we are all personalized expressions thereof, you can also pray and meditate to uncover the answers within that you seek. Only the images change. If you fancy yourself an agnostic, prayer and meditation may seem trivial or unimportant to you; however, introspective thinking can help you solve problems and find answers to your questions. This form of "deep thinking" is a close cousin to the meditation process.

My point is two-fold: (1) the answers are within and not on the outside and (2) everything that is, or will be, is first a thought—the result of creative thinking.

It is reassuring to know, as Napoleon Hill states in his book, *Think and Grow Rich,** "Whatever the mind of man can conceive and believe, it can achieve." It is equally nice to realize that within our creative mind process is the power to unachieve or uproot unwanted "past achievements" that no longer are desired. Not everything we have manifested works for our ultimate good.

We are working with a very receptive medium that dwells within. The study of Mind Science is the study of how thought becomes form. Creation does not mean the making of something out of nothing. Thoughts are things. They are real and creative. Out of them comes everything that is. Everything found in the physical universe was first an idea— a thought in Mind.

*"Think and Grow Rich" by Napoleon Hill © 1963 by Napoleon Hill Foundation, Charleston, SC

CREATIVE IMAGINATION

Do you want more money? A better job? Radiant health? More love? Plant the seeds of success in your mind and rev up your imagination! Your imagination, properly developed, is a super source of inspiration. And there is no stopping a person glowing with inspiration and the desire to win.

William Blake called imagination "the bosom of God." He fervently believed that imagination was one of the most precious gifts man has ever received. The great mental wizard, Albert Einstein, said, "Imagination is more important than knowledge." Think about that for a minute!

A person can turn his life around one hundred and eighty degrees through the understanding and application of creative imagination. Within the marvelous word "imagination" is the powerful word IMAGE. Before the mind can put the creative mental process in motion, it first must conjure up the image or vision of the idea that then will flow from the mental channels and create the outward expression.

All forward motion and progress in our world's history has been the result of creative imagination. Through the faculty of creative imagination, finite man is linked with Infinite Intelligence. To learn how to think is to learn how to live, and to learn how to enhance and fully develop your imagination is to learn how to live life gloriously.

We have all heard the expression "you are what you eat." While there may be some truth in that saying, to a much greater extent, *you are what you think.* What you believe about yourself will become fact. Train your imagination to always look for a "silver lining," to create positive images and not negative ones. When negative thoughts try to creep into your mind, cast them out with positive affirmations. Think about the beauty this world is enriched with. Think about how you can make more money with your bright ideas. Think about love. Think about friends. Think about all of life's magnificent opportunities that wait for your discovery! When you think of these things, all negative thoughts will be unable to penetrate your imagination. Isn't life great? Aren't you excited about the new adventures and opportunities that await you? What a pleasure to be alive, to be able to feel your aliveness and know the creative power you control. What joy, what an adventure and what a blessing life really is. *Can you feel the spirit inside you?*

UP YOUR CONSCIOUSNESS

To achieve "Total Success" and live the life that is powerful, loving, healthy, happy, abundant and self-fulfilling, people must elevate their consciousness. High consciousness is "Total Success Consciousness." It is built on the "I CAN" mentality! The person with the dynamic "I CAN" self-esteem, who also adds much love, faith, joy, peace, helpfulness, honesty and a big dose of thankfulness is the kind of person life smiles on and rewards. He or she is also a person who is attracting rewarding new experiences, effortlessly and constantly.

MENTAL DISCIPLINE

To be the person you were intended to be, you need to exercise some mental discipline. Millions of thoughts, ideas, images, data and suggestions are constantly being filtered through both our conscious and subconscious minds. Nothing is carved in granite, but thinking does make our reality. Mental discipline begins with a conscious effort to obtain and maintain a positive mental attitude. If you're like most people, you have invested (and therefore wasted) a lot of time and effort thinking and worrying about the negative happenings of the past and potential problems of the future—even though 98% of the things we worry about never happen.

It will not be easy to reprogram yourself for success—at least not in the beginning. However, the results will more than justify the mental discipline required. Also, once you consciously work on a positive mental diet for a period of time, soon your powerful subconscious mind will respond beautifully to the positive food you are feeding it, and faster results will be forthcoming. Soon, very little conscious effort will be required from you, although some degree of vigilance is always called for to let the negative thought patterns know they are unwelcome in your mental house.

POSITIVE AND NEGATIVE IMAGES

It is my belief, based on a searching study of "the human condition," that negativity can only survive in a climate void of the positive. Positive thinking always has the power to overcome and "cast out" negative thoughts. A mind filled with "can't do" thinking is a mind overburdened with thoughts of lack, limitations and low self-esteem.

Throw open the mind's door and pitch in some positive thoughts! Watch the unhealthy thoughts disappear. Even a little bit of a positive mental attitude will force some of them out, and when you graduate from a spoon to a shovel and cram in the life-enrichening positive thinking in huge servings, lack, limitation and all of their downtrodden friends will be leaving in droves.

Positive thinking, knowing the inner truth about who you really are (a powerful human being filled with spiritual, mental and physical energy), draws success to you like a magnet. Success means many marvelous, positive things. Success can mean personal prosperity, a fine new home, vacations, travel, a new car, plenty of money in the bank and your money working for you through financial investments. It can mean a business of your very own, expensive clothes, travel and other things associated with material wealth. Success can mean increased love in your life, better relationships, peace, harmony, loving mates, children and friends. It can also mean freedom from worry, more self-respect, self-satisfaction and personal freedom. Total Success can include everything mentioned above, plus even more! Success in all your activities is what you want and is exactly what you deserve!

The law of life is the law of success. You're so much more than you think you are. Once you begin to realize your fabulous potential, there will be no stopping you.

Everything starts in Mind. The only ceiling that has ever been put on your personal expression and ability to achieve EVERY worthwhile goal you want to achieve has been a self-imposed one. Now is the time to blow the ceiling off your self-expression!

The bad news is that we have ladened ourselves with lack, restrictions, limits and "I can'ts." The good news is that we can change our minds and thereby change our lives. You really "CAN DO," and it's important you believe this!

Life responds to us and expresses outwardly the same thoughts we hold within. A modern computer represents scientific achievement. It has great capacity to produce results. So too must we fill our own biocomputer with positive images and data so that it produces positive results.

To learn how to think is to learn how to live. To learn how to live—truly L-I-V-E—is to be a Winner in this wonderful game called life!

"The truth [about yourself] *will make you free . . . "*

—JESUS

*"You were born with wings,
why prefer to crawl through life?"*

—RUMI

Chapter Three

DESIRE

Success is never the result of wishful thinking, but true desire attracts success just as bees are attracted to fresh honey! Seldom is dramatic success accidental. The man or woman who achieves great things is the man or woman who has the ability to think BIG and desire BIG! Desire + systematic action propels one toward success. Anyone can do it!

Success prosperity is an awareness of the treasures life is anxious to give. The word "prosper" actually means to flourish, to win success, to thrive; to experience favorable results. Each person's measure of prosperity is individualized and in exact proportion to his or her drive to prosper. To prosper does not necessarily mean to make a huge amount of money, although making money is one of the best byproducts of the prosperity consciousness. Total prosperity is an absolute. It causes one to experience success at every level of experience. Your personal success desire, if it is in high gear, will spur you on to making prosperity your reality.

TAKE PERSONAL INVENTORY

Success is getting what you want, and happiness is wanting what you get. Success and happiness—key ingredients to Total Success—is a combination of both. My point is simply this: "Be absolutely certain that the things you desire are what you really want present in your experience. The following example of a Los Angeles businessman illustrates this point well.

Brad owned and operated a successful import business for years—a small but prosperous business run by Brad, his wife Kristy and their two daughters. Only two non-family members were employed. After five years of operating this very lucrative family enterprise, Brad got a vision and a consuming desire to greatly expand his successful operation.

In addition to importing sunglasses and magnifying glasses from Taiwan, Korea and Japan and distributing them in Southern California, Brad decided to import many other products from these three Oriental nations. He would distribute them nationwide, throughout the U.S.A.

Soon Brad had to lease a 60,000 square foot warehouse to stock and process the toys, flatware, cameras, projectors and other items pouring in from the Orient. From two outside employees, Brad graduated to over one hundred. From a 35 to 40 hour work week, Brad and Kristy were now required to work 65 to 70 hours a week.

Every February Brad and Kristy were accustomed to a relaxing three or four week holiday in Acapulco, Mexico, but increased business demands now prohibited this type of extended vacation.

Within two years Brad was making twice as much money as he had ever made, but he wasn't happy. His desire to establish a large world-trade import business had helped create the reality, yet the reality was not satisfying.

Brad was able to sell out his toy and appliance divisions, and the family gratefully returned to the small, 5,000 square foot warehouse/showroom where they resumed limited sunglass importing and distributing for only the Southern California market.

Brad's statement to me sums up his experience: "My desire to run a bigger, more expansive import business became a reality. However, the increased time and effort my wife and I had to devote to manage and direct our big new business did not make us happy."

Don't make Brad's error. Put your desire only on things you REALLY want. How are you to know? By taking personal inventory of yourself! An in-depth personal inventory will allow you to decide exactly what you want, and know in advance how your life will be affected when you get exactly what you want.

A FIVE-PART SUCCESS AFFIRMATION

Your desire must be married to your purpose; then add faith, perseverance and a thankful heart. This is how to turn desire into manifestation.

A Five-Part Affirmation for Success
1. I know exactly what I want.
2. I want it sincerely.
3. I know that it is mine.
4. I exert every possible effort to obtain it.
5. I now give thanks, knowing what I desire is mine to enjoy.
   AND SO IT IS!

THINK BIG—DARE TO DESIRE MUCH

Can you imagine yourself a millionaire? This should not be too difficult. Today, even conservative banks and savings and loan associations loudly proclaim that their various Individual Retirement Accounts (IRA's) can help people forty years of age or younger, become millionaires by the time they reach retirement age.

Recently, I read a financial institution's advertisement that proclaimed their investment program could make any customer of theirs a millionaire in just twenty years.

For centuries, the dream of becoming a millionaire has danced in the heads of Americans of all ages. The good news is that now the dream is much closer to reality for many Americans. The bad news could be that a million dollars no longer will equal true wealth. Inflation has taken its toll. Five to ten million dollars in assets is now a realistic goal of today's enthusiastic wealth-builder. Why not be really rich?

Robert Schuller, pastor of the grand "Glass Cathedral" in Garden Grove, California, and television minister to millions, tells this "inflated" story:

A man was shipwrecked and stranded on a desert island for twenty years before he was rescued and returned to civilization. Upon returning to the States, he made a long-distance call to his financial advisor and asked how everything was. The advisor gave him this news: "Your home has appreciated in value and is worth twenty million dollars, and your stocks and bonds also have skyrocketed and are worth over thirty million." The man was elated. "I'm rich beyond my wildest dreams," he proclaimed. Just then, the long-distance operator cut in and said, "If you wish to talk three more minutes, please deposit one million, one hundred and ten thousand dollars and fifty cents . . . "

Thank God inflation has not reached these proportions yet. Still, the man or woman who desires riches nowadays must dare to desire wealth that transcends inflation. They must choose prosperity and abundance, knowing they can have it all by letting go of poverty-consciousness.

BE A BIG DREAMER

Some authors who write on "success subjects" admonish their readers to "stop dreaming and start doing." It is important to put desire into action, but to be filled with desire in the first place, we must be dreamers. The reason is obvious: In order to build the fire of desire, we must fuel it with a beautiful big dream. Action can only be motivated by the flames of desire, which are ignited by the vision presented in the dream.

This changing world belongs to people with big dreams. Life is demanding new technology, new inventions, new ideas and new and better ways of doing things. The leaders in business, science, the arts and politics will be people with big dreams who have the desire to materialize them. Without big dreams, people would still be dwelling in caves.

A burning desire to be, do and have, coupled with action, is the launching pad for the successful dream. Dreams preceed desire, but without desire they are impotent. Dreams without direction only float about in the formless, mental atmosphere and find no channel of expression. A raging desire, interlocked with a big success dream, is a powerful force that takes on an energy of its own. This energy will help the dreamer reach the desired goal. Don't underestimate the power of big dreams, and don't ever stop dreaming.

THE POSITIVE PHRASES OF SUCCESS

About the same time as a great new idea explodes in one's mind and we begin to feel the groundswell of desire, we come under assault by the forces of negative thinking, armed with all their defeatist phrases. Thoughts can have either an uplifting or depressing effect on our success drive. Positive thinking is fed by the words and phrases of victory and success. Negation is maintained by the words of defeat and failure. Big thinkers full to the brim with strong desires are masters at creating magnificent images in their minds. Both silently and verbally, they choose their words and phrases wisely, always replacing the negative with the positive. Do likewise and you will soon see tangible results.

In the left-hand column below are examples of the types of phrases which cause or retain depressing thoughts that may rob us of our success, desire and drive. In the right-hand column the same situation is reversed and presented with the positive "I CAN" attitude.

Negative	Positive
I can't	I can
I won't	I will
I doubt	I am sure
I fear that	I am confident that
I'll wait and see what happens.	I'll make it happen
It's no use, I'm beat	I cannot be beaten
It won't work.	It will work
The economy is against me	I can do it
The times are bad	My time is now
I don't have the time.	I'll make the time
I'm too old (or too young)	My age won't stop me
I don't have the skills	I'll develop the skills
I've tried that before	I'll keep on until I'm successful
Nobody wants my product	People need my product
It's too risky	I'll take the chance
I told you that it wouldn't work and it didn't!	That method didn't quite make it, but I will keep at the idea until I'm successful!

Your own favorite negative responses	The positive replies
_____	_____
_____	_____
_____	_____

By uprooting the negative thoughts and phrases and replacing them with positive affirmations, you will soon be aware of increased excitement in your life. Cultivate your "success garden" starting right now—today. You're going to be amazed at how many weeds (negative thought patterns) you will discover, but don't become discouraged. Uproot them one at a time. And when you notice that you are continually yanking up the same ones, don't be discouraged. Just remember, they often grow in bunches.

At first it may seem like an endless chore, but if you're persistent, you will see measurable results and reap a bountiful new crop. By uprooting the negative and replanting the positive, your success garden will produce a rich harvest. Work at this daily and the results will begin to become apparent in less than one month.

THINK AND TALK POSITIVE
(EVEN IF YOU'RE NOT—YET)

You may be wondering just what the above statement means. Why would a person think and speak positively if his mind was not already tuned in to a positive mental attitude? TO BRING ABOUT THE DESIRED CONDITION, that's why! It's the "Name It and Claim It" game—and it really works!

To be the successful person you were meant to be, you must believe you're that person NOW! You can't be, do or have anything that your mind doesn't first conceive and believe.

Taking this truth one step further, it's not difficult to grasp this concept: by thinking and speaking positive thoughts and words, even before you totally accept the positive mental concept, you will be programing yourself for success. Choose your words carefully. The subconscious mind is the sender of signals to the conscious mind, but it is also continuously gathering data (facts, concepts, impressions, etc.—some true, some false) from the person's living experience. By "forcing", in the beginning, ourselves to think and speak positively, we are feeding our subconscious minds with success food for thought. Soon the subconscious begins to respond and react automatically by sending "success signals" to our conscious mind. When this happens, our automatic, natural responses, words and thoughts will be genuinely positive.

Act as though you are and undoubtedly you will be.

CHOOSE YOUR GOOD

Desire is individualized, and so it should be. Although we are individual beings, we all share common wants and needs that make us interdependent. However, we all also desire specific experiences. You cannot live in a choiceless world. To live without making choices is to forfeit your unique individualism, your very freedom.

We have every right to choose what we wish to experience. We have the right to select the kind of people we wish to be associated with, to choose the city where we will live, the type of work we shall perform, the house we dwell in, the church we wish to attend, etc. There can be no true individuality without prerogative.

Desire can be highly individualized. No two human beings are exactly alike. It is mentally healthy for us to make clear choices. Regardless of your present condition, age, etc., think about what you would like to be, have and do. Forget about any limitations. You may be able to produce one hundred and one "good reasons" why you cannot be the person you want to be, have the things you desire and do the things that would make you happy. All the reasons why you "can't" may be very logical, but just forget about them for a few minutes. Take paper and pencil and make a list of all the choices you would make if you were free and unrestricted to make them. Write down everything and anything that comes to mind. If some of your choices seem silly and unrealistic, that's okay. Continue the exercise. Use the following page in this book, or you can use a separate piece of paper. Work on your list for the next ten or fifteen minutes and then return to this book. Don't put it off. This is an important exercise. DO IT NOW! Be spontaneous. Write down everything and anything that you can think of.

I WOULD LIKE TO BE:

I WOULD LIKE TO DO:

I WOULD LIKE TO HAVE:

Now that you have completed this exercise, it's time to analyze what you have written.

First of all, if some of the things on your list correspond to events and conditions already in your present experience, congratulations! This means you are actually living some of your desires. Nothing is more satisfying!

If, on the other hand, nothing or almost nothing on your page corresponds to your present experience, don't feel alone. Nearly 80% of the people who engage in this little self-discovery exercise do not list one single thing that they would like to be, do or have that is a present reality.

There are only two reasons you can't be the kind of person you want to be, doing the things you like to do and having the things you want to have. They are:

1. You don't believe you can be, do and have
   and/or
2. Your desire isn't strong enough to produce the results you would like.

Desire is a powerful success force, but it will never overcome a person's belief system. A person can desire many good things for himself, but if he does not believe they can be his, they won't be. Desire unfulfilled is very frustrating and causes a good deal of resentment and tension.

Return to your list for just a moment. What would happen if you gave up all the good reasons why you can't do the things you want to? And make no mistake, your list contains many things that you really want for yourself! I know, you would probably have to make some changes, and we humans sure don't like to change. Perhaps what you want to do would require a career change, which first may require new skills. I know, you're too old to return to school, but what if you did it anyway? Or who said they wanted to dance, sing or act? You know that's unrealistic. What if you did it anyway? Or you want to write a book? Come on, that's only for professional writers. What if you did it anyway? And who desires a sports car or a new boat? Do you think that's a practical investment? What if you did it anyway? And what's this stuff about wanting to go into business for yourself? You know that's real risky in these unstable times. What if you did it anyway?

If you do it, if you do the things that you want to do, you're probably going to be happy, energetic and satisfied. You really don't want that to happen, do you? There are no limitations to the mind except self-imposed ones that we accept and hold on to.

You may ask, "What about the really wild desires on my list?" I remember one guy challenging me by saying, "So you think I can be anything I want to be, hey? Well, I would dearly love to play professional football. The problem is I'm not in the best of shape and I'm fifty years old. I simply can't do it."

What the mind can conceive and believe, it really can achieve. However, some of the desires we may fantasize about would take a gigantic and powerful belief system to materialize. If your list contains some desires that you can't even comprehend achieving, you won't. Now don't cop out. Anything on your self-discovery sheet that even remotely seems possible is worth going for. Belief plus desire can make it happen!

Don't give up on yourself or your choices. And by the way, a fellow named George Blanda played pro football with the Oakland Raiders well into his fifties. I guess he never told himself he couldn't do it.

Your desire fills you with enthusiasm and your enthusiasm is your key to the golden door of glorious experience. Choose what you wish to enjoy, for what you desire and place your attention upon will surely be yours.

*"You better not compromise yourself,
it's all you got."*

—JANIS JOPLIN

*"More things are wrought by prayer
than this world dreams of . . . "*
—ALFRED LORD TENNYSON

Chapter Four

FAITH

To obtain faith we must become believers. To hold faith we must believe that all is well. To keep faith we must allow nothing to enter our thoughts that can weaken this mental attitude.

Although faith is maintained by our beliefs, it transcends our belief system. Our belief system changes as we move through life. It is our faith that should remain unshaken and constant.

Faith begins with a belief in God—however you may perceive the Divine (Universal Intelligence, Spirit, That Which Is, the I Am, etc.).

If you're one of those people who just cannot come to terms with any concept of God, you may want to substitute the word Life. It is the author's viewpoint that it is desirable and enriching to come to terms with the Universal Source of all that is, which I call God, but I realize for some this is not easy. Therefore, insert the word or words here that you are presently comfortable with. It's nice to know God doesn't care what name you use. At least I don't think He does. It seems to me, the important thing is that we cultivate faith.

WHAT IS FAITH?

Faith is power. Any thought that faith is only concerned with the religious experience is an erroneous one. While faith may find its highest expression in the spiritual experience, it is not limited to religious practice. The woman or man who is filled with faith in his own abilities will always accomplish much more than another who has not developed faith. A person who has great faith is a person of awesome power. Faith is the force behind belief. The person with faith is not just exercising great power because of what he believes in but because of his belief. Never underestimate the power of the true believer.

St. Paul almost single-handedly took the teachings of Jesus and spread the Master's gospels from one end of the globe to the other. More recently, a fanatical true believer named Adolph Hitler converted a great nation to his dream of world domination and plunged much of the world into a war where millions were injured or killed.

Total faith is total power. It is the zenith of belief. It is an instrument for good. However, if misused, it can bring negative results.

We should always increase its presence in our lives, and at the same time, use it only for the good, the positive, that which benefits all. Any other corrupt use of this force can be destructive to many, especially to the one misusing the power.

FAITH DESTROYS FEAR AND ANSWERS DESIRE

The faith we want to build is the faith that transcends all fear. The faith that knows the positive always is able to conquer the negative. This kind of faith brings into manifestation the good that was first a thought in our mind, and it is the kind of faith that knows our desires will become our reality. True faith believes in things not yet apparent in the physical world, for it knows they shall be reality. Ernest Holmes, in the great metaphysical classic, *The Science of Mind,* tells us, "Faith is the substance of things hoped for, the evidence of things not seen."

The principle governing faith is that the man or woman of great faith is absolutely convinced that their desire will be manifested. This is what is meant in the religious saying, "The answer to prayer is in the prayer itself."

If our prayers are answered in direct proportion to our faith, we need not pray more but rather make certain we completely believe every word we utter. Results are connected to the quality, not the quantity, of our words.

WE LIVE IN AN ABUNDANT UNIVERSE

It is our nature to desire ever-increasing abundance in all good things. We want love, joy, peace, health and prosperity. It is not only good to want your needs supplied but also right to desire the luxuries life is so anxious to provide. How can anyone look at this world and see anything but abundance? It is impossible for us to count the grains of sand on a single beach. Likewise, astronomers cannot count the number of stars in the heavens. Limitation is a word unknown to this universe. Lack and limitation, therefore, are manmade conditions. Surrounded by infinite abundance, too often we dwell on thoughts related to scarcity.

The law of life is the law of success. The universe is limitless but responds individually to our thoughts. If we lack faith

* *The Science of Mind* © 1938 by Ernest Holmes, Dodd, Mead & Company, NY, NY

and restrict our good by holding dear those negative thoughts that instill in us a low self-esteem, we will be oblivious of the infinite abundance surrounding us. Nothing is true or false in the subjective plane accept what we believe is true or false.

The Universal Truth is that to be alive is to be immersed in abundance. But if our present state of mind is centered on lack and limitation, this becomes our personal reality. Nothing will violate the laws of Mind. What we choose to believe in will be our reality. Good and evil are manmade concepts in this universal sense.

Our expression then is not that we consciously choose lack and limitation because we desire personal restrictions, but rather we experience restrictions to our full expression because we are not exercising our faith in abundance and our inherent right to share unlimited beauty, power and riches. The best way to build faith in abundance is to increase our awareness of the Universal Principle of expansion. It is the nature of life to increase and become more. Contraction and becoming less is an unnatural state, contrary to the Law of Life.

Total Faith is unshakable conviction; it is the acquiescence of the mind, the embodiment of an idea, the acceptance of a concept and the visualization of the reality.

HOW TO ACQUIRE FAITH

A house divided will fall. A mind divided is filled with confusion and self-doubt, two major obstacles to acquiring faith. The person desiring Total Success needs great faith. To develop faith he must keep himself in a state of "mental well-being," a state of love, poise, peace, awareness, confidence and equilibrium. Only in this way can he develop the power and "knowingness" that symbolizes faith.

Good mental housekeeping is essential if you are sincere about cultivating great faith. When a negative thought creeps into your mind, the first few minutes are crucial. Do not give the limiting and restricting negative idea time to fester and grow into a real mind sore. Cast it out immediately! It only takes these baby dragons a few minutes to secure a toehold on your consciousness. Never contemplate false suggestions— kick them out of your mind at once!! Soon, your word (and your positive mental image) alone will radiate so much authority, the little creepy negative ones won't dare violate your mental space.

It is inspiring to contemplate the mental attitude of people who are unafraid to have faith in their prayers, dreams and desires. The mastery and force behind the "I CAN" philosophy is the "I KNOW" statement of faith. Human misery is the direct result of fear, ignorance and an "unloved" feeling. Only faith, knowledge and love can free us of this bondage.

Faith builds upon faith. Have faith in your own faith. Have faith enough in yourself to believe you can accomplish your goals. Think about those things you already are fully committed to and have faith in: God, your spouse, your ability to perform a certain task, etc. A little faith is better than no faith and is an excellent foundation on which to build greater faith. Faith is such a powerful principle, you don't need too much (although it is wise to always seek more) to accomplish great things. Jesus taught that a small amount of faith (like in a grain of mustard seed) is sufficient.

If you have faith enough to consider developing more faith, you have enough belief to start with. If you had no faith, you would not be reading this. A Chinese proverb rightly states, *"A thousand mile journey begins with a single step."* Likewise, an invincible pyramid of faith is built one stone upon another.

To acquire faith, it is first of all important to believe you can. **HAVE FAITH IN YOURSELF!**

KNOW YOU ALREADY HAVE ARRIVED— VISUALIZE!

The distance between where you are and where you aspire to be can seem so far at first glance that you cannot imagine reaching your destination. However, there is no real difference between imagination and what we label reality. What you imagine does exist, if only on the mental plane. That in itself makes it possible that it will eventually become a physical fact. Look around your world and all the physical *stuff* within it. Understand fully that everything you see was at one time only a thought. This includes the house you live in, the clothes you wear, the car you drive in, the streets you drive on, the factory or office you work in, the newspapers and books you read, the motion pictures, video tapes and television you watch, etc.

Since we do become what we think, and because everything that is, first was a creative thought, it is vital to our success goals that we now see in our mind's eye the goal accomplished and the journey completed. Visualize this at the same time you start moving in the direction of your goal.

To be, have and do what you want, practice visualization. Visualize in vivid color. Start with a general mental image and then fill in all the details. Paint your success portrait lavishly on your mental canvas. Imagine it so clearly that it becomes easy to imagine. It is already reality. See it so clearly that you actually BELIEVE it is now yours. You can almost touch it! When the conviction becomes so real that you fully accept it and claim it as yours, it will not be very long before it manifests in your experience. It's the "name it and claim it" mental game, and it works! Whatever you want, first see it as already yours.

Adelaide Bry in her fascinating book, *Visualizations*,* tells that you can improve your health, expand your mind and achieve your life goals by directing *the movies of your mind.*

Catherine Ponder's experience also points out another wonderful success principle. To win success, get involved with successful projects and successful people. Help others and you help yourself.

FAITH IS ACCEPTANCE

So often it is easy to forget that all things are rooted in faith. Even those of us who seem to have the most difficulty applying the law of faith in our daily lives can soon uncover innumerable instances in which we accept it without reservation.

We express faith that the sun will rise, that the earth will continue to spin uniformly, that the stars will hold their place in the skies. We demonstrate faith every time we cross the street, drive a car, ride a bus or fly in a plane. We express faith in hundreds of daily routines that we take for granted.

*VISUALIZATIONS: Directing the Movies of Your Mind © 1978 by Adelaide Bry, Harper & Row Publishers, New York, NY.

We have complete faith in the food we buy at a supermarket and prepare at home or in the dinner served to us at a restaurant. Little or no thought is given to where it came from, or more importantly, what chemical and physical reaction it brings to our body. We accept and use it with perfect aplomb. We constantly take our own existence for granted, often planning events years in advance. We express blind faith in hundreds of mundane ways, and yet, too often, we are suspicious concerning faith in the less tangible areas of human experience, from whence comes our every experience.

All human beings unconsciously demonstrate faith daily in their lives. How greater and more beneficial our demonstration when we consciously apply this magnificent principle. Our subconscious is basically reactive. It does not reason inductively. It reasons deductively. Whatever data on the premise is fed into it is acted upon. It is its law to manifest that which it is told. Thus, thoughts are transformed into things through the mental process that turns ideas into reality. Our outer conditions and forms are a reflection of our inner thoughts and mental concepts.

Obviously, all of our thoughts are not manifested into objective reality. A person is capable of thinking many hundreds of thoughts in a single minute. If the Subconscious Mind were to turn each one into reality, the effect would be chaotic. There is a degree of selectivity involved, and herein lies the seeds of success or failure. The subconscious acts upon that which it perceives as constituting a person's strongest belief. The selectivity of the subconscious is directly influenced by the amount and/or intensity of the data being fed in from the Conscious Mind. Thus, negative thoughts (experienced from time to time by even positive people) that are quickly and systematically kicked out of our consciousness have little or no effect on the subconscious. It is when thoughts of lack, limitation and low self-esteem are allowed to remain with us consciously, that they soon seep into the subconscious and then automatically work against our good. Conversely, positive affirmations soon channel into our subconscious and become our number one success ally.

Subconscious mind waits only to serve us; however, we may consciously self-direct. It knows not of right or wrong, good or bad but responds to the impressions we press upon it. The greater the intensity the impression carries, be that "Life is wonderful, new, rewarding, and abundant opportunities are mine to experience" or "Life is a constant struggle; it's a dog-eat-dog world." Choose wisely what you program into your marvelous, but passive, Subconscious Mind. WHAT GOES IN—COMES OUT!

For example, let's use as an illustration that you have decided to be a successful business person. Before you begin to make important decisions regarding your business activities, you could affirm: "I will be successful in business. I will provide products (or services) that people want and need, and I will be richly rewarded for supplying them." It is this positive general affirmation that starts you on the road to success. Once begun, you would continue making affirmations, more specific in nature, to meet each business challenge.

Now, let's present this hypothetical situation. You buy a quantity of merchandise, only to discover that when you offer it for sale, it does not sell or sells very slowly. A "natural reaction'' could be that you have made a mistake. This may be quickly followed by the thought that you are about to lose a lot of money. Now you are really getting upset, and your mind is being bombarded by negative thought missiles. Soon you could be visualizing a total business collapse. Carrying the dilemma one step more, you now have envisaged yourself falling into bankruptcy. What have you done? You have accepted an effort to sell some goods that did not result in an immediate success and allowed your thoughts to concentrate on failure. As long as you uphold this negative programming, your failure will become increasingly more inevitable.

Success is a state of mind. You can't be successful while contemplating failure. No one ever failed by thinking success. No one ever succeeded by thinking about failure. It is just as simple as that, and faith is the powerful substance that keeps doubt and fear from sabotaging our good.

Returning to our example: rather than wallowing in a sea of despair and negativity as soon as the product did not get a favorable reception, a business person needs to demonstrate his or her acceptance of faith. The goal is to provide the goods to a receptive market and to be paid handsomely in so doing. Casting out all self-doubts and failure-inducing thinking, the correct affirmation is: ''I discover the best markets to sell my merchandise and I prosper.'' Correct thinking, of course, must be followed by affirmative action. You search out new channels of distribution. First affirm, then take action! TREAT AND MOVE YOUR FEET!

In a study of successful men and women, this author has discovered most often success was obtained in areas originally planned for. Refuse to accept failure and be open to new avenues that will produce desired results. Always know that within every apparent failure is the seed of greater opportunity and ultimate victory.

BE A BELIEVER

Faith makes miracles possible. It is easy to be a non-believer and self-doubter, but what's the payoff? A life not fully expressive! Remember: THE LAW OF LIFE IS THE LAW OF SUCCESS. People filled with faith are never beaten, never losers. They may lose a battle now and then, but as long as they keep the faith, they will never lose the war. Or, should they actually lose a war, they will bounce back to overcome, recover and claim ultimate victory.

A great example of this ability to rise above all conditions is the German people. Bad judgment and fanaticism on the part of misguided leaders have resulted in resounding defeat in two world wars. In World War II the German nation was bombed into near oblivion. Yet today, in West Germany, the German people have risen to great economic recovery and prosperity. Japan is another shining example of an industrious people determined to overcome. Certainly perseverance is a key factor here, and so is faith!

Faith is a state of mind. It is symbolized by great courage. Every man and woman throughout the ages who helped mankind reach new heights was a person who kept the faith.

Belief in God is said to be the highest expression of faith. Throughout the ages, religions have taught humanity to have faith, but not *how* to have faith. The truth is now apparent:

faith is developed by affirming success and denying anything in opposition to it, regardless of one's concept of God, Infinite Intelligence, or First Cause. Faith is attainable by anyone who can comprehend the creative nature of mind. Faith also grows stronger as one builds success upon success.

Once a person makes the personal realization that thoughts are real things, it is easier to understand that positive thinking is essential in order to obtain favorable results.

The negative always retreats from the positive in all aspects of living, just as darkness retreats from light. Negativity is a lot like darkness—a condition that appears real but is not. Darkness can only fill a void where there isn't light. Fear, doubt and disbelief have no power other than that which we give them. Enter faith, courage and belief and watch them disappear.

Acquire more faith (everyone starts with some) and always THINK YOU CAN. The following popular verse describes how the mind works. It sits on my wall, facing my desk. I read it over often. It may be helpful for you to do likewise.

YOU CAN IF YOU THINK YOU CAN

If you think you are beaten, you are.
If you think you dare not, you don't.
If you like to win, but think you can't,
it's almost certain you won't.

If you think you'll lose, you're lost,
for out in the world we find,
success begins with a person's will—
It's all in your state of mind.

Life's battles are not always won
by those who are stronger and faster.
But sooner or later, the person who wins
is the person who THINKS HE CAN.

*"Change your thinking
and you will change your life . . . "*

Chapter Five

SUBCONSCIOUS MIND—
THE GREAT DOER

Your Subconscious Mind transforms thoughts into things. It is forever working—active all day and all night. Your Subconscious is the architect of your experience. It is always expressing, producing, reproducing and manifesting according to the dictates of your conscious thinking, feelings and core beliefs.

You can use your Subconscious to bring you more wealth, more happiness, more joy and more healthful living by learning to contact and use the unlimited power of your subconscious mind.

This chapter presents the techniques and tools you need to make your life a masterful experience. The person who learns to program his subconscious for success shall never want for anything. Deep within your Subconscious lies the wisdom of the ages, unlimited power, endless resources and supply for everything you could possibly require, all eagerly waiting for the "call to expression." By tapping into this infinite power source and using it constructively, your life will soon be richer, grander, more loving and more joyful. Let other men explore outer space; for now we will explore the Mastery of Life, inner space—*the GREAT SUBCONSCIOUS.*

THE GREAT POWER WITHIN

The silent computer within, your Subconscious, can reveal to you everything you need to know at any moment of time to provide you with the enlightenment to choose the correct path and make the right decision. To benefit from this great power within, you need only be aware and receptive. The new concepts, images, thoughts and ideas are all stored there. Unlocking the golden door to this vast wisdom can enable you to establish new enterprises, create new inventions, write plays, books or songs, develop new art or make thrilling discoveries in any field. Of even greater importance, this power within can be used to find your perfect place on this beautiful planet and allow you to express yourself fully. The keys to the kingdom are available. Total Success is yours if you contact, channel and objectively use this infinite knowledge that has the power to create.

It is your God-given right to go within, acknowledge and consciously use this inner dwelling power. If you approach it with a pure heart, a clear mind and a desire to only use it for your good and the good of others, you will reap the abundant benefits, and so you should!

I have seen the great power lift people out of abject poverty and thrust them forward to million dollar success. I have also witnessed this marvelous force raise people out of crippling states of illness and make them whole again, strong, happy, vital and well.

This great power source, combined with the unlimited power of love, can create a perfect relationship or heal one that is in danger of falling apart. It can bring people together. It can make life worth living.

WHAT IT IS AND HOW IT WORKS

Now that we have mentioned the marvelous results that are obtainable in consciously using and directing our Subconscious Mind, let's investigate how it works and what it is.

Your subconscious is your servant. It receives messages on the mental plane and acts upon them. Your wish is its eternal command. Your Subconscious mind serves you by manifesting your beliefs. It can only act on the law of belief.

All of your thoughts, experiences and acts have been stored here. Your Subconscious knows you better than your best friend, lover, parent or spouse. It knows you far better than you consciously know yourself! Your Subconscious mind is both knower and doer, but it only acts according to the signals you send it and according to your belief. It is always busy turning your thoughts about yourself into your experiences. Unconcerned with finite concepts of good and bad or right or wrong, it simply wants to turn your thoughts into things and conditions. It only desires to serve you.

Any student of Mind Science soon realizes there is only one Mind. You have but one mind, but your mind possesses two singular characteristics. Each distinct characteristic is unique, with separate attributes, functions and powers. These two aspects of mind are often referred to as the Objective and Subjective: the Conscious Mind being the awake or objective and the Subconscious being called the sleeping (although it really doesn't sleep) or subjective. What appears to be a duality—two separate minds—is simply two separate functions of the One Mind.

The Conscious Mind of a human being is constantly acting and reacting to stimulus in the outer world. It analyzes and often passes judgment on circumstances, events and experiences. It makes an association of pleasure or pain, conjures up feelings of security or insecurity, happiness or sadness, good or bad with every experience it perceives as meaningful. With every expression it records as meaningful, an impression is left. The Conscious Mind responds to the senses. It is an instrument of sensation, a thing that relates to this world and responds to this world. Primarily, the Conscious Mind is a recorder, an analyzer and a filer of information and stimulus. It is preoccupied with perceptions and feelings. Pain or pleasure (physical, psychological and emotional) make the strongest impression on it. It is masterfully capable of self-direction, but too often is preoccupied with the effects of the outer world.

Without self-direction your Conscious Mind can and will send all kinds of different signals to your Subconscious. Some are bound to be positive, others may be extremely negative. Left without a "positive screen" that prevents the negative from entering, you may be planting weeds and thorns instead of grapes and figs, and what your Conscious mind plants in the soil of your subconscious, the subjective will busy itself with turning these "mind seeds" into full blossom.

When a person learns to think positively and abundantly, the thought seeds deposited in your Subconscious Mind are loving, harmonious, peaceful, confident and fully self-expressive. The Subconscious then produces a harvest of beauty, joy and abundance. We have already stated: to learn how to think is to learn how to live. Controlling the data sent to the Subconscious is how to achieve a more rewarding life by controlling our thoughts.

Why aren't more women and men expressing joy, health, wealth, happiness, peace and power? Take a little time to observe the people you come in contact with. Soon you will be aware that most people live in and at the effect of the outside world—the world without. Only the more aware and enlightened men and women are students of the Mind and the world within. If you will look increasingly more within and put these principles to work, your life will be transformed and new power and joy will be yours. Remember, it is this inner space, the world within of thoughts, imagery and the creative process, that molds and shapes the outer world. The outer world is effect, the inner is the Cause. To change external conditions you must go directly to Cause. Most people fail to reach their goals because they attempt to change effects by working with effects. It is impossible to do. You can chop down the weeds in your garden, and even enjoy this effect for a very brief time, but unless you go directly for the root, they will soon return. Change is always at the level of Cause, never at the level of effect.

THE LAW OF MIND

While the conscious mind of man is knowing, self-assertive and has volition, will and choice, the Subconscious Mind is the Law of Mind in action. It is the channel of all thought. Its function is to turn thoughts into things. It is the *"middle medium"* between cause and effect.

This Law of Mind is such a powerful force that it is easy to think of it as an entity in and by itself. It is not. Its subjective state only acts when set in motion by data received from the conscious. Once put into action, however, it exercises its inherent power to create the effect that will correspond to the thoughts it has received. It may produce freedom or bondage and worries not about what humans consider to be "good" or "bad". It is the great doer, and it does do what it is told. The Law of Mind is subjective to the intent of man. The Conscious, wise use of this Law can bring you unlimited wealth, love, joy and other blessings. But like any other energy force, misuse its vast powers and you suffer the consequences. We are dealing here with two Supreme Principles: Love and Law. It can truthfully be stated that we live in a loving Universe that upholds success but does not violate the Law. Your Subconscious Mind acts as a mirror. It molds your convictions about yourself and your thoughts about your life and casts them into your reality—multiplied! It knows not how the effect will be judged. Its deductive nature acts on the message, whatever the message is that it receives. The Law of Mind obeys the orders that it is being given by your Conscious Mind.

It may be wise to point out here that although it is called the Conscious Mind, that side of the mind that is objective and relates to the objective world, it is capable of processing both conscious and unconscious data, images, feelings and impressions. Without good mental housekeeping, the Conscious Mind can be sending negative signals and feelings to the subconscious, totally unaware of the seeds it plants. No one consciously chooses lack, limitation, misery or bondage, but they are "natural" results of a prolonged negative state of mind, personified by the Subconscious, which acts to manifest the thought patterns it receives, regardless of what type of conditions it will produce.

We must fully comprehend the Law of Mind. We are not dealing with a reluctant Force but one that is entirely receptive, actually compelled by its nature, to receive the images from your thoughts and act upon them.

POSITIVE USE OF THE LAW OF MIND

The positive application of using the Conscious Mind to program the subconscious mind to bring the success we desire begins with Mind Control—*taking control over your own mind!* Much pain, suffering and havoc have been wrought by those who would control other people's minds and thereby dominate them. Ultimately, this unnatural lust for complete power over others is self-destructive. True power and ultimate success are achieved when you take dominion over your own mind, thereby exercising self-direction in your life. What you think is what you become.

When you think correctly and speak the words of truth, beauty, love, riches, health and bliss, the Law of Mind will respond and deliver these harmonious conditions. By Consciously controlling your mind, you can apply the powers of your Sub-Conscious mind to any problem or difficulty you face.

The pearl of unlimited potential is within. The greatest power source in the universe lies just beneath the surface, and it's yours to use to win unmeasurable success. Stop programing yourself for failure. Don't say, "I can't do it; I can't afford it, etc." Say instead, "I CAN DO IT; IT IS MINE." The Law of Mind acts upon your true beliefs. Affirm the positive and it can only produce positive results. Believe in the power of your subconscious to fill you to the brim with self-esteem, love, health and prosperity. It is your God-given right to live life richly, and your Subconscious Mind will make that fact your reality!

The natural tendency of your Subconscious is to allow you to be more self-expressive. Although passive by nature, in-bred within it is the desire and energy to help you achieve your goals. If you but give it a little direction, it will carry you the rest of the way. Feed it just a few heart-felt, positive affirmations and watch it go into affirmative action. Plant the seeds and it will produce the harvest. Proof of the Sub-conscious Mind's ability to maintain order for us is evident in all our body functions. It is the Subconscious that is the guardian of the body and all our biological functions. It has been said, "The Subconscious is the builder and keeper of the body." When one is able to comprehend this amazing service performed by the Subconscious, it is easy to under-stand why many New Thought teachers feel that the only reason positive affirmations are required is to erase all the negative affirmations we have heaped upon our Subcon-scious.

Positive thinking is a tool to obtain positive living. The Self-Actualized person who is already living life to its highest expression need not seek what is already his. His expression of life is his constant, living, positive affirmation, and his subjective nature knows nothing that is opposed to this living truth.

You may have noticed that you haven't reached this state of High-Consciousness. Most haven't! Some may be reason-ably close to this exalted state; many others still have much of the journey ahead of them.

The important thing for us to know is that WE ARE ON THE PATH! And if we have erroneously laid some false mental barriers across our roadway, let's use all the positive weapons in our arsenal to drive them out. Don't worry, they always retreat without a fight once we send in the positive forces. Someday we may not have to be concerned about a positive mental attitude, but for today it is the tool that helps us reach our destination. Bless it, give thanks for it and USE IT!

THE BOTTOM LINE IS RESULTS

Many people fail because they misuse the awesome power that is their Subconscious Mind. Two principle reasons for failure are (1) lack of self-confidence and (2) energy spent trying to change things at the level of effect. When you begin to comprehend Mind Science, your confidence and self-esteem dramatically increase, and you know change can only be at the level of Cause. The bottom line is results, and results are only possible at the level of Cause.

Never forget that your Subconscious Mind is subjective and not objective. It is the doer, not the instigator. When it accepts an idea as our true intent, it immediately begins to materialize it. The Mental Law is activated and all resources and energy combine to manufacture the reality. This mighty power is willing to work for good or bad ideas. Consequently, if it is used unwisely or negatively, it can produce failure, disharmony, confusion, destruction and ultimately defeat. Consciously applied, it brings freedom, guidance, peace, love, health and wealth.

It is not difficult to discern what constitutes wise, constructive use of this power. You need never fear misuse if your thoughts are centered on loving, positive and life-expanding concepts. You must immediately reexamine your premise when your thoughts relate to "taking something from someone else," "having power over another" or any other strategies that come out of fear, mistrust, jealousy or other forms of unwholesome thinking. Deep within ourselves is a knowingness that always can discern the positive from the negative. We gain much when we learn to seek and listen to its wise inner-counsel. This intuitively wise Source has been called a person's I AM SELF, The Divine Self, or simply, your Conscious.

We must learn to trust our feelings. Wisdom transcends intellectual knowledge. The sincere student of Mind soon discovers the importance of intuition and the rich rewards and right decisions that are obtainable by listening to the Inner One. Feelings are signals that can guide us. You have heard the much repeated quote "if it feels good, do it!" More and more behavioral scientists, psychologists and Truth-seekers are discovering that this statement, like so many other cliche, is basically accurate.

WILL POWER ALONE WON'T WORK

Will power and determination are admirable qualities. Will power, in several situations, may be used as an effective success tool, but it alone won't produce success. Many books have been written about will power, sometimes implanting the impression that it is the paramount ingredient that makes achievement possible. This is nonsense! Your Subconscious Mind does not respond long to coercion. Self-directed will power can aid us in repelling negative thoughts. It is, in a sense, an effective extension of courage. The problem with relying too heavily upon one's will is that the will is an effect of Mind—a positive effect—but still an effect.

Don't misunderstand. Developing more will power may help you overcome undesired habits. The will is a close cousin to courage, and courage is fathered by Faith. Human will power is an instrument of success but not the source of success. It can be a condition of positive, powerful living, and a favorable condition, but still, it's a condition. The problems that rise out of undisciplined use of human will power are associated to the human inclination to attempt to overpower outward effects and conditions. This is misuse of the will and Mind Power. You can fight conditions forever and not be victorious. Fighting conditions will only leave you battle-scarred and tired.

Proper use of the marvelous tool that is will power is in the steadfast knowing (Faith) and confidence in yourself and your success strategies. This keeps you centered and leaves your will unshaken by other people, events and conditions. The will power in tune to the positive goals does not fight real or imagined enemies or try to crash down the door of success. Self-directed will power is constant in purpose and confidently keeps us moving in the right direction. However, Mind directs the will and not visa-versa.

89

UNDERSTANDING THE MENTAL LAW
OF REVERSE RESULTS

The famous French psychologist Coue defined the law of reverse psychology over 50 years ago as follows: *"When your desires and imagination are in conflict, your imagination invariably gains the day."*

Here's an example:

If you say, "I want a better job, but I can't get one," "I try very hard to find one," "I use all the will power I have, but it's no use," you have short-circuited your goal. The Subconscious Mind cannot act against a mental condition that is dominant. Your will power and desire are doomed to failure when they confront mental images that are locked in to deeply implanted conditions. Success is a force that flows. You can't force success, but you can get yourself in the stream of things and go with the flow.

The reason we often obtain results that appear to be the absolute reverse of the good we hope for, pray for and will to receive is because somewhere implanted deep within our Subconscious is an imagined condition that says, "I can't have it," or "I don't dare believe it." We have been told, "Know the truth and the truth will set you free." This means we must uncover and excommunicate false negative mental ideas and replace them with life-expanding, positive ideas. Cause and Cause only can change effects. Hope is better than despair, and having will power is better than not having any, but until a negative mental condition is driven from our subconscious by a positive one, real change cannot occur. To employ mental force against your problems is to

90

pre-suppose that the Mind can be a battlefield in which the forces of success must combat the forces of bondage. Just as darkness vanishes where light shines, without fighting it, so too will the negative disappear when replaced by a positive belief.

Speak the words of success and back them up with unswaying conviction and you'll be victorious. To fight against your problems is to become weary and discouraged. To recognize them as false conditions that always flee the truth is to defeat them without ever firing a shot.

Mental coercion results in fear and anxiety and will not produce favorable results. Speak the words of success and be certain they are backed up with belief and convictions that give them energy. Talk is cheap, unless it is coming out of a state of mind that embodies faith, conviction and commitment. Saying that you see yourself "making large sums of money" at the same time your thoughts are centered on your bills, your lack and your poverty-stricken condition is an exercise in futility. Only by seeing the negative state of affairs as a temporary deceptive condition, unsupported by anything but a false mental premise, can we dissolve it and replace it with the correct mental equipment. The positive is always supported by the Law of Life because THE LAW OF LIFE IS THE LAW OF SUCCESS! Never forget this truth!

NAME IT AND CLAIM IT!

In computer operator jargon, "GIGO" means "garbage in—garbage out," indicating the mechanical wonder of advanced technology is still at the mercy of the living programmer. Such is the truth concerning our Subconscious Mind. What comes out of our mind is what we first put in it. Are you shoveling in "garbage" (negativity) or "precious bullion" (Total Success Mind Food)?

Where we place our attention is what will come forth. Ernest Holmes wrote, *"Whatsoever we identify with, we tend to become."*

A black minister in New Orleans, Louisiana, recently wrote, saying, "I was born into a very poor family who lived on the outskirts of New Orleans. My father was always telling my mother, me and my four brothers and sisters, 'If you're born poor, uneducated and black, you don't have no kind of chance in this world.'

'I knew I was born poor, and there was no question I was black. I enjoyed school in my younger days, but I knew my daddy would expect me to quit school when I reached age fifteen to help him share-crop the five acres our family leased. By the time I was nearing fifteen I was resigning myself to the fate of an uneducated poor man with no kind of chance in this world. Then something unexpected happened. My father was offered a better job at a factory in the city. Overnight the family income increased, and we left the farm and moved into a small city house. Daddy still thought it would be a good idea for me to drop out of school and find some work, but just as I reached the legal age to quit school, my mother spoke up for the first time in her life. 'James isn't quitting school,' she sternly told Dad. 'He's going to get himself a fine education and make a better life for himself, his children and our grandchildren. God doesn't want black folks to be poor and uneducated.' I was allowed to continue high school, and thanks to both a grant and my folks help, I attended college for four years. I became very successful in the business world for many years before I decided to do God's work. Now I tell everyone in my congregation that they can be successful regardless of skin color or what conditions they were born into. Through the grace of God, you can pray for it and claim it."

This inspirational story illustrates that we need not be at the mercy of conditions but rather can take dominion over all conditions in our lives. This moving story also points out the power of both negative and positive affirmations. You're self-defeating when you affirm "I don't have a chance." It is always the "I CAN DO IT" attitude that makes success possible and probable.

WE GET WHAT WE EXPECT

Life may or may not give us what we want. Life always gives what we expect. What are you really expecting? Hopes, dreams and "I would like to's" are great, but what do you *expect*? What do you really conceive as your experience? If you're hoping to open your own business and make big money but don't expect it will happen, you're right, it won't! If you dream about acquiring new skills but think that it is too late to teach an old dog new tricks, you're right, it is! If you would like to have more friends or maybe form a love partnership with that special person but can't see it happening at this time, you're right, it won't!

You may now ask, "I have heard that expectations can cause us anxieties and stress." As Terry Cole-Whittaker so lucidly pointed out in her book, *What You Think of Me is*

None of My Business,* "Others are not your source . . . as we think that what we want emanates from others, we become frightened. We come to believe 'they are withholding,' and we seek to placate them to get what we think we need. That's what dependence is." This is expecting our good from others and not from our own Creative Source. We are always expecting some form of results. The anticipation of positive results helps create the reality. Just like the Bible says, "It is done unto you as you believe."

Begin now affirming and expecting—but not demanding—only positive, life-enhancing, richly rewarding conditions and experiences. You deserve it all: Love, health, money and happiness and every good experience. You're a unique, one-of-a-kind special creation. As the pop saying goes, "God don't make no junk!"

Expect favorable results and watch them manifest in your life! You have no idea how good you are. As you become more aware of your awesome, latent powers, you will accomplish more than you ever dreamed possible. Let's rid ourselves of our excuses! Make God, not other people, your source and expect favorable life-enrichening results!

WHAT'S YOUR EXCUSE?

Social workers, welfare employees and others who work in the ghettos of our big cities find people of all different ages, religious beliefs and education backgrounds living there. These tragic souls represent a cross-section of humanity. Poor education and lack of marketable skills may be prevalent, but surprisingly, many people on welfare who live in the ghetto are not uneducated. Although unsimilar in

---

**What You Think of Me is None of My Business* © 1979 by Terry Cole-Whittaker, Oak Tree Publishers, La Jolla, California

several respects, most people of the ghettos have one thing in common: They have an excuse, often a very good one, why they are not productive members of society. Some blame the color of their skin or their ethnic background as their major stumbling block. Others give lack of skills or insufficient education for their plight. Still others will tell you what a "raw deal" they have received from certain other people or society at large. Show a little interest and they will gladly tell you their story. They usually will present a convincing tale of woe, filled with "valid excuses" why they have totally failed.

Leaving the ghetto and moving uptown a little, or moving out to the immediate suburbs, we find ourselves in the dominion of the neighborhood of the great "middle class." Mr. and Mrs. Middle Class live much better than the people of the ghetto. Some of these people are actually happy and self-fulfilled. When that is the case, God bless them, for that's what life is all about.

Too often this is not true. The middle class of this great land, collectively, are not a happy and satisfied lot. To be average and mediocre and "in the same boat as the Jones's" is not a great self-esteem builder for many. Often, Mr. Mediocre feels threatened by both the rich and poor. He often feels he does not enjoy the same advantages or "loopholes" coveted by the wealthy. At the same time, resentment has built against supporting the have-nots.

Mr. Middle Class usually is able to keep afloat, just barely, but too often the joy of living is absent. Jealousy for the rich and anger associated with high taxes paid to support the poor are not conducive to a state of joy, tranquillity and happiness. He, too, has a story to tell. His excuses are many and usually "very reasonable." Too often he clings to his story when to release it would free him to go forward and excel!

As we climb upstairs into the uncrowded heights of big success, we find men and women from all walks of life. A few were born with the proverbial "silver spoon" in their mouths. Many others began in the ghetto. Most were once a part of the vast middle class. The successful also have a story to tell, an exciting story on how they made it big. Here there are few excuses—at least not financial ones.

I hasten to point out that financial success is just one, albeit significant, aspect of Total Success. The nice thing about achieving financial freedom is that it will free you to turn your attention and the power of Mind onto life's other important experiences. Being materially rich will not, in and by itself, make you happy. It will simply give you one less challenge to contend with, providing that you understand the laws that govern wealth and use your treasure wisely.

What's your excuse? We are innovative beings. Whenever we fall short of complete success in any endeavor, it is not hard for us to seek and discover a "good reason" for failure. The trouble with excuses, even the best (logical) ones is that they are a poor substitute for success. Living by and with our excuses is anything but rewarding. Forgive the pun, but they really are a poor excuse for not being a winner.

What if you gave up your excuses? What if you shed them all and no longer carried them around with you? If you will let go of your story about why you did not win success, you can write a new one. Your new story can be the greatest story that you ever lived. The choice is yours. You can't keep your excuses and have success too. When one is present, the other is always absent.

YOUR IDEA BANK

You have probably heard someone say this about another who has created a huge fortune: "The lucky guy. He got this great idea and it made him rich." While it is true that good ideas manifested are the core of all success, it is very erroneous to think that one is lucky to get a great idea or that there is anything haphazard or accidental about the flow of creative ideas.

Chance has absolutely nothing to do with great ideas. Creative ideas are attracted to the creative thinker. He attracts them by maintaining a mental position (subconsciously and consciously) that pulls ideas to him like a magnet.

Great ideas are available to all. The magnificent stream of Universal Consciousness is forever flooding our minds with imaginative new concepts. Our own self-constructed mental barriers are the only way we can block this natural flow of illuminated thoughts.

The answer is always in the question. If we will but ask the question and believe, the answer will shortly arrive. The power is always available; the idea is always anxious to present itself. The creative goals of human beings are always to do something new, better, greater, finer, more helpful, and yet, we spend so much of our precious time upholding mental positions that attract negative thought patterns, so firm is our misplaced faith in lack, limitation, suffering and failure.

The possibilities to acquire great ideas from your subconscious mind are endless and imponderable. Our task is not to create great ideas but to be receptive to the positive ideas that we are submerged in. To do this we must clear away the debris and remove the barriers. There is nothing to get that is on the outside. Everything is within and awaits only to be beckoned.

Faith is the key. Free yourself to ask the aspiring question. With complete faith, the answer is available and will come. If you want to start a new business, get a better job, take a trip, buy a new home, find a life mate, create a new invention, write a book or uncover rich new investments, ask this question: "How can I accomplish this worthwhile task?"

Don't struggle to find the way; know the answer will come. Don't worry and doubt; have confidence and believe! Soon, within an hour, a day, a week or a month, the answer will be revealed to you. It may come from the silent voice within, or it may come in the form of a seed that slowly but surely begins to flower. Don't doubt it will come, and don't try to force it. Only believe it will come. All things are possible, but only to those who believe. You won't have to work hard to get the answer. In fact, the only work required on your part is to remove all obstacles (negativity) in the path of the answer. The key to your idea bank is your faith in yourself and your heartfelt desires for more creative expression. The Subconscious Mind has stored unlimited ideas and also is the medium for transmitting your desires into their physical or monetary equivalent.

In the process of turning the desire into the deed, action on your part may be necessary. God helps those who help themselves. However, no effort is required to produce the brilliant idea. Just faith.

Getting an idea involves opening your mind to it, with total trust that it will come to you. Faith is the answer: Faith in Creative Intelligence and faith in your own God-given abilities. The answer is available. The idea will come.

Once an idea becomes evident, you may have to exercise discernment before implementing it. Your Idea Bank is capable of giving you an idea that is tailormade for immediate use in a perfect "as is" state, and this is not always the way it will work.

Often, like a rough, newly minted diamond, an idea will require some polish and preparation. It may need patient examination and some refinement. Your task may be to alter it from its broad general design into its most individualized and utilitarian form.

Through examination, prayer and/or meditation, you will become clear on how best to implement your basic idea. The greater your faith, the clearer your vision. The stronger your desire, the deeper the impression upon your Subconscious, and the sooner the anticipated results.

If your idea was conceived in love, for advancement, to create, to help, to enhance, then prosperity and success will be yours as it manifests itself. You need not try to rush it, hurry, worry or even work hard for it. When your faith is strong and your treatment positive, everything required for success will fall into place. If certain additional skills are required, how to obtain them will become clear. If other people are needed, they will begin appearing in your life. If money is needed from outside sources, it, too, will become available. Whatsoever is needed to put a good idea into action is always available. The Subconscious Mind knows the how and the when. If we just give it our true success intention and remove from it previous negative programing, it will do the rest.

Infinite Intelligence is available to you. The unlimited power source and creative energy in the Universal Subconscious is the power source for your own Individualized Subconscious mind. That's a lot of power. The most powerful energy source in the universe. Use it wisely.

"Get what you want out of life.
No one can make you feel inferior
without your consent."
—ELEANOR ROOSEVELT

"The way is the goal"

—LAO TZU

Chapter Six

GROW WITH GOALS

A goal is an objective, a purpose, a reason to be in the race! Far more than just a dream, it is a visualized objective that is being acted upon. A goal is not wishful thinking, it is thought-channeled on definite purpose. No positive forward action can be taken until a goal has been established. Nothing great is possible without the setting of a goal.

If you want big success in any and every worthwhile endeavor, YOU MUST SET B-I-G GOALS!

It isn't important who you are or where you have been, it's where you are headed now that will make you or break you. You're headed nowhere without goals; or as one modern philosopher observed, "Without goals, you could reach your destination, but you would never know it."

The author believes in BEING HERE NOW and living in the here and now. If you started this book from the beginning, you know how I feel about getting "stuck" in the past or spending too much time being concerned with the future. Life is always Now.

The beautiful thing about the setting of goals is the forward progress you experience in the here and now as you move toward your future objectives. Just as a glorious vacation provides great pleasure enroute to a destination, so too with goal setting. We can experience joy and personal satisfaction by being on the path. In fact, getting there can be just as rewarding as arriving. Anticipation is exciting!

Making resolutions, especially on New Year's Day, comes easy to people. A resolution that is not backed with unyielding Faith and Desire is little more than wishful thinking and is not the same as setting goals. The reason 98% of people's resolutions are abortive is because behind them is a lukewarm mixture of hope, willpower and wishful thinking. The "I hope I can" or "I would like to" mentality is not conducive to powerful goal setting and ultimate goal achieving. Only dynamic, positive statements, backed by mental convictions, followed by right action can produce uncompromising results. Replace wishy-washy intent with affirmations of "I AM," "I CAN," "I DO."

VISUALIZE YOUR GOALS

People who teach themselves to use the power of creative visualization continually produce amazing results and build an impressive track record of achievements. Any desire firmly held in your mind and consistently tied to forward physical action tends to become objectified in form. The form may be something that is readily seen on the physical plane, such as a new house, a fine car, a new boat, jewelry, money, etc., or it can be an attitude or condition, unseen, but no less real. The manifestation of attitudes, conditions or quality of character could include perfect health, new friendships, a satisfying love relationship or a better job. The mind is very receptive to visualization. Because of this truth, we should use broad strokes and bright colors to paint a grand picture across our mental canvas.

FROM A "BUG" TO THE BEST

I know a real estate salesman named John who drove an old, beatup, ten-year-old Volkswagen. His top goal was to own a new Mercedes Benz. To help the power of visualization along, he not only pictured a beautiful new Mercedes in his mind's eye, he also clipped several color photographs of his dream automobile from ads in magazines. These clippings soon adorned the visor of his VW Bug, were pasted to his bathroom mirror and above his office desk. He even put one on his bedroom closet—the first thing he looked at as soon as he awakened.

First year real estate salesmen are not expected to make a lot of money, especially in a real estate market plagued by high interest rates and a sluggish economy. Lots of well-meaning folks told John he would be lucky to list and sell a few homes just to make ends meet. John thanked them for their advice, totally disregarded it and kept looking at photos of a new Mercedes while visualizing himself behind the wheel, tooling around Southern California.

At the same time that over sixty percent of real estate sales people, newcomers and old pros, were dropping out of the profession, John sold over one million, two hundred thousand dollars worth of real estate and earned himself sixty thousand! Guess what? He is the proud owner of a new, white Mercedes. He not only bought this beautiful automobile, he paid cash for it!

John achieved his goal and immediately set a new and even bigger one. He has been clipping car photos again to paste up on his closet door, in his office, on the mirror, etc.

On each photograph is a magnificent—yes, you guessed it—Rolls Royce! The car he wants sells for well over fifty thousand dollars.

Lots of people are telling him he is crazy to expect to own such a car. "John, why can't you be satisfied with your beautiful Mercedes? It is one of the world's finest luxury cars!"

John's answer is simple. He will tell you he loves his fine Mercedes, and he still wants a Rolls. "It's my new goal," he says.

I, for one, will not bet against John. He knows all about goals and how to achieve them. He also knows the importance of setting a new goal to keep him moving forward.

Our goals may not center around luxury automobiles. They are nice, but there are many marvelous things in this majestic universe, tangible and intangible, worth setting goals for. Take your pick! Just remember: Whatever you desire, keep it in your mind's eye.

GROW WITH YOUR GOALS

Five-year plans are nothing new to business. Economists and investment analysts are fond of five-year growth and investment projections. In the world of professional sports, coaches, managers and team owners—especially those of *losing* pro football or baseball teams—are forever coming up with "five-year rebuilding programs." Too often, the results of the fifth year of their programs aren't much better than the first. A five-year program, be it in business, investment, education, sports or any other activity, is probably the maximum long-range time for planning. However, favorable results are only obtainable when definite goals are set and vigorously pursued. Any program that merely projects "hoped for" results is doomed from inception.

Here's a worthwhile exercise for the serious goal-setter. Visualize your own five-year plan in these five departments: (1) Work, (2) Investments, (3) Home, (4) Social, (5) Education. Make a commitment when setting five-year goals. Answer all of the following questions. Be clear, precise and certain.

MY FIVE-YEAR PLANNING GUIDE
(and my answers to the following questions)

(1) Work (business) 5 years from today
    (A) What income level will be mine?
    (B) What responsibilities will be mine?
    (C) What satisfaction do I expect from my work?
    (D) Will I start a new business, expand my present business or continue to work for another?

(2) Investments (wealth) 5 years from today
    (A) What net worth will be mine?
    (B) What investments will I pursue?
    (C) Will I be financially independent?

(3) Home life 5 years from today
  (A) How loving will be my relationship with my spouse?
  (B) Where will my family and I live?
  (C) What kind of home will be mine?
  (D) What kind of vacations will we take?
  (E) What financial support do I want to provide for my children?

(4) Social activities
  (A) What vital causes will I be championing for God, country, and/or my community, myself?
  (B) What type of friends do I want?
  (C) What social groups will I be a member of?

(5) Educational pursuits
  (A) What new skills will I have learned?
  (B) What new skills will I be learning?
  (C) What new hobbies will I have?

KEEP MOVING FORWARD

The self-directed, goal-centered person is constantly moving forward. Movement denotes life, and forward movement is synonymous with goal achieving. When you have no personal goals you are moving to, you will go around in circles or stand still and become inert. In either case you would be retracting from life rather than expanding your living experience. Life always yearns to be more, know more and experience more. Any retreat from this natural form of expanded expression is unhealthy and unrewarding.

GOALS INCREASE YOUR ENERGY

The man who has to drag himself out of bed each morning to face "another hectic day of work" and who limps through the day has goals far below his potential. Great goals put enthusiasm into living and give a person an increased energy supply.

The person who always seems to have an unlimited supply of energy is an individual who is an enthusiastic goal-setter. This woman or man has a grand vision in mind and is eager to jump out of bed and get active in the quest. People who are forever "struggling with life" soon burn out. They become bored, uninterested and uninteresting, beaten and very tired. Eventually they give up. Have you noticed how many "tired people" there are?

When life is reduced to a struggle, you are bound to get tired and brow-beaten. Life is too big to struggle with. The tide is too powerful to go against. You either go with the flow or you don't go! Resisting life can only bring self-defeat. BE ENERGIZED BY LIFE, BY SETTING REALISTIC BIG GOALS, AND THEN GET GOING WITH THE CURRENT.

KEEP YOUR GOALS CONSISTENT

When it comes to goal-setting, B-I-G is better. Your goals will serve you best if they are large-scale undertakings and at the same time consistent and compatible. They also should be realistic.

Setting a goal of owning a new Mercedes or Cadillac when working as a shoe salesman at six dollars per hour is not a realistic goal. The Mercedes or Caddy is not an unreasonable objective—many thousands of people drive them, and so can you! You just need a realistic approach, such as a job or business that allows one to make as much money as he is capable of making.

There is nothing wrong or demeaning about any kind of work: sales clerk, cook, bank teller, factory worker, etc. It is simply unrealistic to make huge sums of money in certain professions. Other occupations offer more opportunity.

Owning your own business, of course, allows you to make as much money as your talent and service will allow. Selling careers (direct marketing, real estate, insurance, etc.) also help take the ceiling off your earning power.

If some of your goals are related to "expensive things"— homes, boats, cars, jewelry and other luxury accessories to abundant living—you must first set a goal to have the "ways and means" to make it all possible. To have expensive things, (and you do deserve them) first find the best money-making strategy.

A goal to own a beautiful, $400,000 beach-front home is perfectly correct, and it is attainable. If our present income is not compatible with such a lofty dwelling, we simply must set an immediate goal to uncover the right kind of job, investments or business opportunity that will help make our future goal a reality.

A friend of mine did just that. He changed careers three

years ago. He gave up his accounting practice and entered direct marketing with a line of health-food products. His income went from $35,000 a year to over $200,000. He loves his big home on the beach!

TO GIVE YOUR GOAL ITS BEST OPPORTUNITY TO SUCCEED, MAKE YOUR GOAL BIG AND PRODUC- TIVE, PLUS REALISTIC AND CONSTRUCTIVE!

Set your goal high and challenging enough to stimulate your creative nature, but also construct it so that you really can believe in it. Set short-range or intermediate goals to reach longer-range goals. Long-range goals may be more meaningful and exciting to you. To reach them, set short- range goals that are more believable and achievable. Grow and go from goal to goal!

"SEE" YOUR GOALS ACCOMPLISHED

Put the incredible power of visualization into practice. See your goals reached. Don't confuse creative visualization with wishful thinking or daydreaming. Daydreaming is part of your fantasy life, and it can be a fun and positive exper- ience. It is not goal-setting. Wishing is a meaningless, un- channeled exercise that is a result of hoping.

Hope has some mental fiber built-in that, combined with courage, can assist positive action. Wishing is a watered- down distant cousin that lacks creative authority and usually gets "lost" somewhere in the great, formless mental at- mosphere.

"Seeing is believing" is a time-worn cliche, but the Principle of Mind Science works just the opposite. Believe first and you will see it! Do it! Have it!

THINK BENEFITS

There are only two chief reasons why people do anything they do:

1. to gain benefits
2. to avoid losses

Human beings seek to gain something they don't feel they already have, or they want to avoid losing something they perceive themselves as already having.

Mind Science clearly shows that we have it all because within us is the Creation Principle. However, within the realm of human psychology, it is fair to say that humans want to gather additional benefits while holding onto the ones they already possess.

A healthy mental posture is to know that what you claim as yours will not be taken from you. Think benefits! Benefits are yours, not by adding new things, but rather by removing old ideas, restricted thinking and personal negativity. Shed the old winter garment of low self-esteem, limiting thoughts and personal fears, and the real, beautiful, powerful *you* emerges.

You are the prize! Like a beautiful, brilliant diamond, some polishing to remove any foreign substances and outer debris is all that is needed to let your magnificence unfold.

Discard the superficial and unnatural coating and let your light shine!

KNOW YOUR GOALS AND WHY YOU WANT THEM

Creative goal-setting has no kinship with daydreaming and wishful thinking. Wishing our goals into reality is very unlikely. We must speak our word and back it with real faith. Do no wishing. Instead, KNOW. Do no dreaming. ACCEPT. There is no need to get on your knees and pray (although you can if you want to). ANNOUNCE your intention. KEEP THE FAITH and BELIEVE IT IS ALREADY YOURS!

Knowing is a key factor. First know what you want and why you want it. Fully understand your intent behind each goal you seek. Be certain your intentions are always positive and uplifting, for yourself and others who may become involved in your goal. Know your goal is an uplifting experience for all concerned. Carry your knowingness one step further: Know it will be yours!

ACCEPT YOUR GOALS AND THEN TAKE ACTION

Once you know your goal is good, and once you put your Subconscious Mind into action by knowing it will deliver your desire to you, or you to it, accept it as accomplished. Acceptance doesn't mean you sit back and do nothing. There may be, and probably is, much physical action required on your part. Cheerfully go about doing any and all activities called for, and still accept the results as if the goal was already completed.

The architect of a major, modern building knows his work

is finished once his design is completed. It may be several months later before all the work is done and the structure stands, but he knows the resources will materialize his grand design.

Likewise, accept the goal as fact at the very same time you are busy working on it—no doubts anymore, only acceptance followed by action.

ANNOUNCE YOUR GOAL—TO YOURSELF

After you have set a goal to mind and used your mind's eye to visualize it the way you want it, then it's time to announce your goal—to yourself. It is time to make a firm commitment to yourself. You may have a compelling urge to tell others about your great goal, but resist doing so—at least until the goal is already in high gear and the wheels are rolling forward.

Too often energy for a new goal is dissipated by confiding in others. Telling others about your planned project sometimes ebbs the power behind the project. Then too, some people experience so much pleasure in telling others about their great plans that there may be a tendency to dream up new plans rather than carrying their current plan to a successful conclusion.

Announce your intentions only to yourself in the early stages. One excellent way to accomplish this is to write your goals down. Spell out every detail just the way you would like it. Using paper and pen can finalize your desire. It will give you a real sense of commitment. It materializes (on paper) your intent. It is also extremely helpful to write out the entire goal plan just the way you perceive it. Just don't set it in concrete. Be open to any beneficial changes or new avenues that may open up to you. A great goal-setting affirmation is: "This is my goal and this is how and when I want to achieve it. I am open to having it sooner or even better than I have planned!"

KEEP FAITH IN YOUR GOAL

Having faith is a prerequisite in setting a goal. Without faith your goal is unlikely to become fact. It is just as essential that you maintain faith as you encounter challenges along the route—as you most certainly will. If you have set a big goal, your courage, conviction and perseverance will be tested. Know this in advance. Keep the faith, and it will see you through.

BELIEVE AND YOU WILL RECEIVE

Faith will make you a believer, and believers are achievers! All of life's riches are available to the believer. If you can only believe, no one can stop you. Believe and it is yours.

HOW MANY GOALS?

It is important to maintain a singleness of purpose in your goal-setting. This does not mean you cannot move toward several goals at once. You certainly can. Working for several goals at the same time is splendid, providing they are realistic and consistent in nature. Two goals in conflict with each other can cancel each other out.

Interlocking goals (goals closely related to each other) are

115

very productive. Goals also can be fixed to different time-tables and desires. We need short-range goals, intermediate goals and "ultimate" goals.

Let's suppose an "ultimate" five-year goal is to enjoy a six-month vacation traveling throughout Europe. The short-range goal may be to merit a raise in salary or to increase your business. The intermediate goal would be to save several thousands of dollars for the planned vacation over a set period of time, all leading up to the "ultimate" experience as you step into a transcontinental airplane or board a luxury ocean liner.

MORE ABOUT ENTHUSIASM

Enthusiasm is an amazing goal-builder. It is a very beneficial abstract. It cannot be seen, weighed, measured or scientifically defined, yet it is a real thing—a mighty force. It is the energy, the "go-power" that motivates human beings to achieve their high goals. The more enthusiastic we become, the greater our joy in living. To put more enthusiasm into your life, begin to see your life as a glorious adventure, filled with exciting experiences and unrestricted potential. This is the truth about yourself!

You have the ability to create a joyous new world for yourself. Nothing good is being withheld from you. You are becoming more successful each day. Your horizons are forever expanding. This whole beautiful world is your playground. The only thing between you and Total Success are a few negative ideas. Look within. Uncover and uproot these false, self-restricting, anti-success attitudes and thoughts.

Let your light shine and the darkness will disappear. Life is the greatest gift—a fascinating adventure. Be here now and enjoy it. Make every day a day of new, exciting beginnings. Release any guilt you harbor. Forgive yourself. Be gentle to yourself. You never did anything worse than make some mistakes. You were less aware then. YOU ARE MUCH MORE AWARE NOW. Forgive yourself and release the past. Set new, exciting goals today and GO FOR IT!

MAKE THEM YOUR GOALS

Don't allow anyone else to choose your goals for you. For desirable results, they must be yours alone, although others may share the benefits. If you are trying to please a relative, spouse, lover or friend in selecting your goal, check your premise. Is this goal really your own heart's desire? If not, your chances of reaching that goal are very slim.

Most of us are unduly influenced, consciously and subconsciously, by other people, especially relatives and loved ones. Their opinions mean so much to us we may actually set goals on their recommendation. Our need for approval is often (usually) too strong. We may abort our own desires and follow another path in hopes of pleasing them. Goals set in hopes of pleasing others usually fail. Such goals that would succeed in other cases where our need for approval is so strong would not be long enjoyed. No person is an island. Our goals will often center around other people and be shaped somewhat within the boundaries of our environment and the society in which we live. Still, they must be ours!

If you're happily married or live with a loved one, mutual happiness, success and self-expression is an important consideration. To move forward together, it will help if your goals are not in conflict. A little give and take may be called for, but never live your life vicariously through another. To do so will eventually lead to identity problems and self-restriction, followed by resentment. To achieve worthwhile goals you must set worthy goals. To enjoy your goals, they must be yours.

A word to the wise. If you're already married ot living with someone and want to remain in that state, some compromise may be the order of the day. However, it is a good idea for each partner to give the other enough loving space to work toward individual goals in careers, education, etc.

If you are not yet lovingly encumbered, it may be a good idea to discuss and consider long-range goals before becoming partners with another.

GOAL EXAM

The purpose of the following ten questions is to rate yourself in ten specific areas to determine which goals deserve priority in your life. We will use a 1 to 5 point system as follows: Very good — 5 points; Good — 4 points; Satisfactory — 3 points; Need improvement — 2 points; Need much improvement — 1 point. Don't think about the number you assign. Complete this exercise quickly. Let your intuition direct you, and be honest!

118

1. Relationships   _____
2. Getting along with others   _____
3. Leadership ability   _____
4. Work ability   _____
5. Money-making ability   _____
6. Awareness of abilities   _____
7. Self-esteem/attitude   _____
8. Spiritual/psychological qualities   _____
9. Education and skills   _____
10. Memory and recall   _____

Now, add your numbers from the above ten questions and fill in the total here: _____ .

This "goal exam," if done spontaneously, should point out the areas in your life that could benefit from immediate attention. If you filled in the number 5 everywhere, you are either in super shape or a liar!

Anywhere you see a 4, only a little attention is needed. A 3 for this exercise is average, but you don't want to be "average" when you can be very good! If you see something less than a 3, you know where to direct your focus. Enough said. And if you honestly filled in 5 points for "very good" to all 10 questions, that gives you 50 points. Redouble your goals and you'll go from 50% (very good!) to 100% (perfection!).

For those of us who haven't quite reached our "perfection" just yet, and do not always express ourselves "very good," take heart. We are on the right path now. If your total points were less than 40, you will simply be on the path longer than some others—and the path to success is definitely where it's at! *SUCCESS IS A JOURNEY, NOT A DESTINATION.*

YOUR GOAL CHART

Now that you are beginning to become aware of where new commitment and goal-setting will pay the richest dividends, use the GOAL CHART on the following page to list at least three "priority goals." Give yourself a Goal Statement, list any obstacles, solutions to any obstacles, an exact time (date) for completion and the benefits you desire.

GOAL CHART

YOUR GOAL(S)	OBSTACLE	SOLUTIONS	DEADLINE	REWARDS	COMMENTS

You may make copies of the Goal Chart (it, along with the following "Things To Do Today" page, are the only two pages in this book that the author gives his permission for you to copy) and use them in your goal-setting. Better yet, use this Goal Chart as a guideline to construct your own chart on a much larger piece of paper. This will give you more room to write.

DAILY GOALS

Any goal-setter worth his or her title not only sets short, mid and long-range goals, they also set daily goals. A daily goal-setter has a lot going for him. This day-by-day practice gives a person the mental discipline to move up to the big "ultimate" goals. Daily discipline puts your Total Success program into synergistic motion. Don't delay another day! Start right now by working with daily objectives. Don't say "I'll do it someday." DO IT TODAY! Use the following page or one similar to it (these excellent daily objective goal sheets are available in most stationery stores or office supply shops) and begin using these sheets daily. The results will amaze you!

THINGS I GOTTA DO
TODAY

Date _____

Done

1. _____ ☐
2. _____ ☐
3. _____ ☐
4. _____ ☐
5. _____ ☐
7 _____ ☐
8 _____ ☐
9. _____ ☐
10. _____ ☐
11. _____ ☐
12. _____ ☐
13. _____ ☐
14. _____ ☐
15. _____ ☐

The idea of a successful life puts your Subconscious Mind to work to create your success. Goals keep you pointed in the right direction. Goals help center your dynamic energy so that you can zero in on your objectives. Going with your goals, including the day-to-day objectives, not only will bring you to your desired destination, they will also make your life on the great pathway more exciting and joyful.

Never stop setting goals. Once one is met, love it and enjoy it and then set another, just a little higher. A string of daily and short-range successes will soon lead you to some mighty impressive, intermediate goals and then on to your really, really big ultimate goals.

What do you do after you have climbed the mountain of success and achieved a big whopper—a super ultimate kind of goal? That's easy—set another monster goal and get back on the path. It's great to pause briefly to enjoy each goal as it is obtained. Pause and enjoy and give thanks. Then get right back in hot pursuit of the next major objective! To stop setting goals is to stop accomplishing things. You never want to do that! Goals keep life interesting and exciting!

We must consciously comprehend that goal-setting puts the creative power into action. The more total our acceptance is of this truth, the more powerful will be our demonstration for definite purposes. Goal-setting is not a passive demonstration in that physical action is usually required. The goal gives self-direction to positive action.

Set big goals that are consistent in nature. They also must seem realistic to you. This means you must be able to believe in them. You may wish to be a rich and famous actor and set this as your goal, but if you cannot accept this concept, you have little chance to make it your reality. While it is possible to have anything you want, to achieve it you must believe you can achieve it.

The person suffering from low self-esteem can build new confidence by growing with goals. A string of short-range and intermediate goals achieved will increase faith in the ability to achieve greater goals.

Goal-setting can make a believer an achiever. Total Success is only possible to a person who works and lives for his or her goals.

For all sad words of tongue and pen
the saddest are these:
"It might have been . . . "
JOHN GREENLEAF WHITTIER

Chapter Seven

APPLICATION AND PERSISTENCE

The majority of people are ready to give up their desires and goals and wave the white flag at the first sight of misfortune or opposition. They surrender too easily when to carry on would make their dreams come true. The old cliche is so true: *"Quitters never win and winners never quit."*

Knowledge is not power. You can only obtain power from the application of knowledge. Application of knowledge gives you the power, and persistence allows the power to produce results and make your goal come true. You can listen to marvelous metaphysical and human potential speakers, hear motivational tapes and read inspirational how-to books from now to kingdom come and still experience no positive forward motion unless you apply what you have learned and then have the *git and grit* (persistence) to see it through.

THE MYTH OF SELF-IMPROVEMENT

Several millions of books are bought each year (some even get read cover-to-cover) by people who wish to "improve" themselves. These same readers, and many others, also attend lectures, workshops and seminars in hopes that they will enhance their lives. From "How to Improve Your Memory" to "How to Dress Better" and from "Weight Reduction" to "Witchcraft", millions seek new ways and means to make their existence more meaningful. Self-improvement is big business in America, Canada and throughout the western world. People desperately want to improve. This concept is myth, even though the intent is valid.

A human being is a creative force with the inbred powers required to take control of his destiny and build his own reality. The living spirit that emerges from his or her mother's womb has, deep within itself, unlimited Universal potential. To state that this magnificent creation, with unrestricted creative abilities, needs further improvement to be more useful or more productive is nothing short of sacreligious. It is this erroneous "improvement syndrome" that can actually impede forward progress. It can make someone think there is something out there to "get". This is not so.

You have it all inside you. There is nothing on the outside you need to get. You have it all. In fact, the only thing you need to get is a sense that all the answers are inside, ready to become apparent.

If this book will help make you realize that you have got it all already and only need to remove the false and negative "barnacles" that your perfect ship has collected over the years, it will change your life forever. You're the precious, one of a kind, original! You're better than you ever dreamed you were in your most self-centered fantasy. Like the highest grade of gold in the best South African mine, only far better, you need only to remove the surface material and the real you—the beautiful, intelligent and powerful you—will emerge in all your radiant splendor. Unlike gold, diamonds or gemstones, there is only one you! Self-realization, not self-improvement, is the answer!

Even the learning of new skills, which would probably be called improvement, is nothing but the application of latent abilities you already possess. Everything we "learn" how to do was first self-taught by another who applied Universal

Knowledge and then exercised persistence to see the application through to completion.

THE MAJOR CAUSES OF FAILURE

You will not fail because you can't do the task at hand. You can fail only because you won't do it. Very few people consciously decide to fail; still, many do fail. Close inspection of failure always points out the two major causes. The two causes of failure are the two big "won'ts":

1. won't try
2. won't continue

You can't be a winner if you won't get in the race, and you can't be a winner if you drop out of the race.

Following is a story that clearly shows the importance of getting in the race and staying in it.

Carl and Kathryn are friends of mine, a couple in their early forties who put a lot of emphasis on physical fitness. Carl got involved in running several years ago while Kathryn just recently decided to trim down by joining her husband on his daily runs along the horse trails of Lakeside, California. Since he had been building his running legs for several years, Carl decided to enter the San Diego Marathon, a gruelling, 26-mile run held annually.

Carl was shocked when his wife told him she, too, would be a contestant. "Don't be silly!" he told her. "It will be a big test for *me*. Why, you wouldn't even last the first half of the race!"

"I'm entering, and I can go the distance," she stated with even greater resolution.

"Okay, baby," Carl teased, "but just try to keep up with me."

The day of the big event finally arrived. During the first two miles of the race, Carl paced himself and was content to run stride for stride with Kathryn. At this point he glanced over to her and said, "I'll wait for you at the San Diego Stadium [the finish line and destination of the runners]. You're going too slow." With a condescending wink, he took off with a burst of motion and soon was far ahead of her, joining the front-runners.

Because Kathryn's goal was in the running itself and also in finishing the race, she continued to pace herself against the fatigue that can overcome any distance runner.

Hours later, as Kathryn continued to run, now crossing Mission Valley, with the stadium in sight, she noticed Carl and another runner sitting on the side of the road. Carl had burned out, and his feet were bruised and sore. Kathryn was about to stop and attend to her husband, but Carl admonished her. "Honey, you deserve to obtain your goal. Finish your race and then pick me up in our car. I love you and I am proud of you."

Later, Carl admitted that he had foolishly spent precious energy by running far ahead of Kathryn during the early stages of the race, and it had cost him during his stretch run. "My ego got in the way," he confided.

Carl is basically a much better runner than Kathryn. He is both stronger and faster, but like the saying goes . . . "Life's battles (goals) don't always go to the bigger, the stronger or the faster. Sooner or later, the person who wins is the person who thinks he can!" Persistence, backed by belief, a goal, proper application and true desire is a cornucopia of powerful ingredients that produces measurable results. This is what makes a goal a reality.

SUCCESS BUILDS UPON ITSELF

Emerson said, "Do the thing and you will have the power." Wise words from a great man. One job finished is worth one hundred partially done. There is a snowballing effect consistent with success. One success leads to another. Success builds upon itself. The correct application and steady perseverance you apply to a "SMALL GOAL" WILL FEED YOUR SELF-ESTEEM AND GIVE YOU COURAGE TO SET AND ACHIEVE BIGGER GOALS. People who fail and then completely give up rarely do so after only one setback. More often it is a string of defeats that compound their distrust in themselves and others, that finally finds them throwing in the towel. No matter how many times you have experienced setbacks, you can now go on and become a goal-achiever. Set a realistic goal and apply the knowledge you have already received from this book. Add persistence and you will achieve. The elevator to success is out of order, but you can still get there—one step at a time!

OVERCOMING OBSTACLES

You probably have already become aware that there are many peaks and valleys along life's highway. Personal planning goes awry, relationships fail to actualize, accidents do occur. Problems or challenges are a fact of life. Since we cannot escape our obstacles, we must face them. The solution is always in the problem. Retreat or inertia is never the answer. Fighting with our obstacles never works. What do we do then? Face them and erase them! Every time things go wrong we have the opportunity to prove and demonstrate the Power in our lives. It is not only what is happening but how we are reacting to it that matters.

Life is great and the curves on the highway make it more interesting as long as we don't allow them to throw us off course. When I moved from Saint Paul, Minnesota, to San Diego, California, several years ago, I made the trip by car, and it was a fascinating, three-day journey. Among the most scenic states I drove across were Colorado, Wyoming and Utah. My journey began by driving across Iowa and Nebraska. I made excellent time crossing these two fine Midwestern states. The roads were good and I faced mostly flat terrain and straightaway motoring. After a day of driving, however, I was frankly a little bored with the scenery, wheat and cornfields, and pleased to enter the rugged terrain and raw beauty that Colorado, Wyoming and Utah offered.

Often I would have to travel at greatly reduced speeds, but each curve in the road, or peak of a mountain, provided picturesque scenery and primitive beauty. I loved viewing nature's living, rugged landscape as I journeyed through those three Western states, and at the same time, I was happy to return to the straightaway driving that was possible as I passed through the desert state of Nevada and into the beautiful Pacific state of California. As I reflected on my journey, I realized the change, diversification and stimulation provided by each state I drove across helped make my trip more exciting.

Life's journey also is fraught with curves and changes, and this can make life more stimulating. By overcoming obstacles and viewing problems as challenges, we can grow spiritually, mentally and emotionally. If you're in life's mainstream and moving forward, you can expect peaks and valleys, change and challenges. Life is never stagnant. Life is never dull. Because life loves becoming more, uncovering more, experiencing more life, it is never totally predictable. Thank God it is not. The thrill of living is in the new, exciting experiences of living. Don't fear obstacles in your path. Journey around or through them or stop long enough and turn an obstacle into an opportunity. They, too, can be stepping stones upon your success ladder. Just never let them stop you and leave you immobile.

MIND SCIENCE APPLICATION

Knowing the truth about our vast abilities gives us a sense of power and new freedom. Still, we must act upon this knowledge in order to reap the benefits. Working hard denotes drudgery and efforting, the need to struggle with our jobs, our relationships, our very lives. There is nothing hard or unpleasant involved in putting the Principle to work in our experience. Mind Science application may require (and usually does) certain actions to be taken on our own behalf. When we learn to love ourselves and love our lives, every action required is enthusiastically performed. Joy is the only way to approach every activity. When joy is instilled in everything we do, even hard jobs become easier and interesting, and unpleasant tasks lose much or all of their unpleasantness.

Once you have conceived a plan of beneficial action, felt the desire and set a realistic goal, application must begin. Not sometime soon, not even tomorrow but right now! Correct application always begins right now, at the very place and space you now find yourself and this very day! Even if you're working toward several objectives at the same time, there is something good and productive you can do today to help each objective.

NOW IS THE RIGHT TIME

The only time we will have to discover our abilities and enjoy our experience is "'Now'', this very moment. How wisely are we using the here and now? Are we trying to re-create the past or are we daydreaming about tomorrow? It is not productive to do either.

Mental acceptance and physical application of all good things for ourselves now gives us the opportunity to build a continuity of positive thinking and positive living.

This does not mean that every moment will be a demonstration of all the heart can desire. We will be challenged from time to time, and outward appearances will not be all that we wish they were. In times of severe challenge and when our emotions appear to be unbalanced, more than ever our pattern of right thinking and right application will guide us quickly through the outer storm. Inner peace can be transformed into outer strength to help us face and erase any worldly crisis.

Undesirable conditions and situations may appear, but to remain in our life we must hold onto them, think on them, talk about them and thereby give them power. To erase them, we should acknowledge only our desire to release them or discover the solution that dissipates them. Don't think about the undesirable situation, think about its cure. Don't talk about the unhealthy condition, seek its immediate healing. Most people who experience a new problem or challenge stop living positively now and begin to think about and wrestle with the condition. If and when you believe in the Mind's ability to overcome matter, you will realize correct thinking yields the favorable answer to any given situation.

Now is the right time to demonstrate your belief in your ability to achieve success. You can demonstrate your power now. Don't put off the application of these proven Success Principles another day. Be renewed and transformed by the power of your mind—NOW!

KNOWING IT IS RIGHT FOR YOU

As mentioned before, the real criteria as to whether a desire should be acted upon is in examination and knowing that it will benefit you and not injure another. If it feels good and will express more life, abundance and happiness, you need not fear misuse of the power of Mind. Even so, it is possible to demonstrate a condition that, while not inherently harmful, is not the truest and best effect for us. By carrying the creative visualization beyond our initial desire, we can actually see ourselves experiencing the goal. Does it feel right? Is it as good as we want it to be? Is it our heart's desire?

An industrial psychologist named Paul knew how to use the Science of Mind to change his life but forgot to consider all the conditions that came with his demonstration. Paul earned an excellent salary working for a famous West Coast human engineering study center. He also made substantial profits from investing in Southern California real estate.

A few years ago Paul decided he wanted a completely different lifestyle. Some friends of his had moved to a farm in Arkansas and were always praising their new "living off the land" lifestyle. Paul decided he, too, wanted out of Southern California. He loved the mild climate but was dismayed by the many thousands of new people moving into Southern California each year. "I need room to breath, space to be me," he declared. He then quit his excellent job, sold all his property and flew to Arkansas. Within a few weeks he had bought a 110-acre farm in a remote area of Arkansas. The nearest "city" was 28 miles away, and the population there was only about 10,000.

Paul's desire and goal quickly became reality. Not one to procrastinate, his application was swift and decisive. Shortly after moving into his big farm house, he sent several of his friends photos of his "spread" and a long letter extolling the virtues of the back-to-nature movement. I must admit, his farm was a lovely-looking place. Hundreds of trees stood on his property, the house was quite old but obviously well-built, and he even had his own lake on the property.

I was more than a little surprised to receive a letter from Paul less than a year later telling me his dream property was up for sale. He had discovered a life of farming was quite different than he had anticipated. He had visualized a lifestyle that had excited him, but the day-to-day chores associated with that lifestyle had not been considered. The solution: He would now sell his farm and move to a suburb of Little Rock, a good-sized city but still very small compared to Los Angeles or San Diego. He would work as a psychologist in his special field, and he would buy a house with a few acres where he could be a *weekend farmer*. He loved raising fruits and vegetables, but only as a hobby—not a vocation.

A very happy solution for Paul. However, he could have avoided a really hectic year of farming over one hundred acres and struggling with the work of a fulltime produce and chicken farm, had he spent a little extra time "knowing if his decision was right for him."

Know not only what you want but also the responsibilities that will be yours when you get it. Look at your objective from all sides. Consider the new responsibilities that will be yours once you manifest your desire. And if from time to time you create something that is not altogether to your liking, that's okay, too. We can learn from everything we do. Bless it, then release it or change it and go on to some other grand new adventure. The foremost thing: Live in the NOW and keep moving forward while applying the Principles.

TEACH YOURSELF PERSISTENCE

With forward motion, a defined goal and the right application, you're almost an achiever. Now let's add a heaping portion of persistence.

Persistence is the embodiment of desire, self-reliance, organized planning, courage, willpower, cooperation, dedication and finally, habit. We can teach ourselves to be persistent.

Perhaps you have been a quitter in the past. You may have left a trail of half-finished projects behind you. Don't worry about it now. Many of us have been in the same boat. Remember, it's what you do about it now that counts. Complete your present task, even if it is not important to you that you do so. A better you starts today, and it starts with goals—even small goals—achieved. We need to build a stable foundation to support us as we climb the ladder to success. Completed tasks and goals accomplished, even small ones that may appear to be insignificant at first glance, help prepare us for greater success and provide us with a solid foundation to build success upon.

Dickens said, "We forge the chains that we wear in life." This simply means that we are capable of doing everything we can see ourselves doing successfully and that we can sabotage our own good—no one else can. The most certain action to guarantee failure is to take no action at all.

DON'T TALK ABOUT IT—DO IT NOW

There is power in both the written and spoken word, and also a price paid in the form of energy spent. A modern philosopher observed that there were three kinds of people:

1. *those who make things happen*
2. *those who talk about what's happening*
3. *those who don't know what's happening*

While I agree there is a real measure of truth in the above saying, I have also observed a lot of folks who fall into a fourth category: people who spend a lot of time talking about what they will make happen. Too often these well-meaning people never follow through with their good intentions, ideas and big plans. We have already discussed the importance of defining our objectives and setting our goals. Having done this, don't spend precious time and energy telling friends, associates or anyone else who will stop to listen, your plans and strategy. Keep them to yourself, at least until the die has been cast and both your thoughts and application have become fully synergized and your persistence has become unshakable. Only then would I recommend that you share your objectives with others.

Of course, certain objectives are apparent to all. If you enter a competitive sporting event or an open contest, your fellow competitors and all spectators will be aware of your intent. Even then, the less said in advance, the better. Your "ground work" for any desired goal is usually best served by diligent preparation and little or no talk.

STRIVE FOR PERFECTION

My Webster's Dictionary defines *perfect* as "complete, indeficient, absolute, impeccable, unblemished, flawless, faultless, blameless, infallible and pure."

Now, that's a tall order to live up to, but one worth striving for. Only when we put our very best into our Mind work will it satisfy us. There is no deliverance from low self-esteem and negative thinking patterns without mental conviction centered on perfection in all that we think, say and do.

To assert our unique individuality is to transcend the law of averages. To consciously apply abundant life thinking in all areas of our experience is to put unlimited mental power and law into action for our good. All forward evolution of a person depends on his conscious cooperation with the Law of the mental universe. The world we live in may appear to be flawed, blemished and very fallible; nevertheless, by fixing our attention on the Universal Principle, which is perfect in its application, all things become new. Mind is forever ready to materialize exactly what our thinking is centered on. This is our link to infallability. This is the perfect power that makes striving for perfection the highest goal and not just Pollyana thinking or an impossible dream.

The fact that man has discovered and used perfect application in various scientific endeavors is indicative that perfection is not impossible. Cosmic flashes of illumination have also inspired men and women of the arts to produce masterpieces. This very same power has inspired literature which is filled with pure genius and lasting value. Now, in this New Age, the time is right to strive for perfection in our work, in our relationships and all other activities. When the finite unites with the infinite, all imperfection will disappear.

PERSISTENCE BRINGS GOOD LUCK

Some people believe "luck" determines who obtains success and who doesn't. Actually, it is the application of faith, desire, courage and all the other Mind Principles that attracts good luck to us like a magnet, provided that we have the persistence to stick to it and work toward our goals.

William Shakespeare, a pioneer in the philosophy of "applied luck" made available through persistence, wrote, "If it be not now, yet it will come." The readiness is all! The literary master's words have profound meaning, for the effort that we make to bring our desires into reality can be the deciding factor between achieving good fortune or experiencing failure. Shakespeare also gave us these words on persistence as it relates to specific goals. He wrote, "Determine on some course, more than a wild exposure to each chance!"

The aware person is confronted with new opportunities daily. Opportunities are in abundant supply, and often it seems difficult to choose which to pursue. It is wise to pray and meditate over the course to follow since we must be selective. It is humanly impossible to do everything that interests us; therefore, we should zero in on the goals that best suit our desires and unique personality. Once a goal, or group of goals, is put into motion with self-directed application, it is our persistence, and persistence alone which can lead us to a successful conclusion.

What may at first appear to be good luck is the conscious application of success laws and the persistence to complete each worthwhile task—and goal. Success fosters more success and soon becomes a habit. When you begin to pyramid success by sticking to your objectives, you, too, will be labeled a "lucky" individual. My friend, Frank Davis, is fond of saying, "The longer I stick at it, the luckier I get."

SUCCESS THRIVES ON PERSISTENCE

The ability to stick to any activity long enough to produce favorable results is indispensable to success. Many fine personal attributes—a fine education, good contacts, a charming personality, etc.—are far less vital to success than the ability to stay goal-directed and persevere. This is what separates the champions from the also-rans!

Don't confuse this wonderful quality of persistence with a tendency to stick-to or hang on to something or someone, even when to do so is destructive. Some plans, conditions, even relationships, should be released and let go for the good of all concerned, especially ours.

Applying persistence to a well-defined goal is indispensable. It is almost impossible to prevent your own success if you stick to it and continue to persist. Don't quit!

It was only a couple decades ago that a milkshake mixer salesman turned one San Bernardino, California hamburger stand into a vast fast-foods empire. That was Ray Kroc, and the company he built is called McDonald's. Mr. Kroc did not become wealthy until he was in his mid-fifties, and he is a strong believer in the following words, and so am I.

Press On!
Nothing in the world can take the
place of perseverence.
Talent will not; nothing is
more common than unsuccessful
men with talent.
Genius will not; unrewarded
genius is almost a proverb.
Education alone will not;
the world is full of educated derelicts.
Persistence and determination
alone are omnipotent.

"You don't have to suffer continual chaos in order to grow . . . "

—JOHN LILLY

*"Our doubts are traitors and make us
lose the good we oft would win
by fearing to attempt."*

—WILLIAM SHAKESPEARE

Chapter Eight

WEALTH IS A STATE OF MIND

Increasing your wealth and having more money can be very good for you.

Money is only one symbol of wealth, and yet it is a very, very important form because it is symbolic of the true riches found everything in the Universe.

You deserve to have money—lots of money—and you can easily be rich. Money is important, and the more you have, the better. The concepts presented in this chapter will help you think rich and get rich. They will give you deeper, more powerful insights into what money really is. Some of you have decided to read this chapter ahead of any others. That's okay. This would only point out how strongly you realize the importance of a "prosperity consciousness". Just be sure to backtrack and read every chapter in this book.

Love, sex and money are words that command instant attention. They are so vital that Total Success requires that we have the right attitude about them. Now, let's turn our attention to the joy of having lots of money—not just enough to get by, but *more than enough* so we can enjoy complete financial independence!

UNDERSTANDING FREE ENTERPRISE

Although perhaps not perfect in all respects, capitalism upholds free enterprise, and free enterprise offers the creative individual far more opportunities than any other economic system. No other system allows the individual to make as much money for his or her talent, service and creative ideas. Totally free economics offer the enterprising individual unlimited potential. A free marketplace operates on supply and demand and encourages and rewards the industrious.

America has a capitalistic economy, but many restrictions, some seemingly for the public's greater welfare, others highly questionable, have been placed on our "free enterprise." Many of the social programs introduced in recent years are socialistic in nature. Too often, such programs, however well intended, restrict individual freedom in the name of helping the less fortunate and less productive. Any system that does not reward incentive and places too much emphasis on poverty is in danger of decline and fall into a state of national poverty.

Humanistic programs that aid the mentally and physically handicapped deserve our support. But any able-bodied person who refuses to work is not helped by assistance. The Bible says, "He who will not work shall not eat." It is this author's belief that rather than help, many of our socialistic programs are robbing those they propose to help by taking away both their incentive and dignity, thereby promoting a state of financial bondage. Lack is a state of mind first; then it's expressed by restricted living. To reward poverty-thinking in able-bodied individuals is, in my concept of self-reliance, counter-productive to the individuals concerned and society in general. I believe great value should be put on self-reliance, and unrestricted rewards should be available to the producers. Research has shown that the greater the perceived value to an individual, the more creative and dedicated will be his effort to obtain it. Society as a whole advances through the efforts of creative, goal-oriented, individually successful persons. Successful individuals create a successful society.

Any notion that the captains of industry—business people—are unethical or not worthy of trust is totally erroneous.

Some businessmen do believe in taking unfair advantage of the public. Such unaware, greedy types are definitely among us. But is this good reason to fault the entire system? I think not! Crooks are crooks, be they dressed in dark-blue business suits, engaged in "white collar" crimes with pen and paper or be they wearing faded blue jeans, using a knife or gun to rob someone. Neither lawless group represents the morals or beliefs of our free enterprise system. Both should be vigorously prosecuted!

By now, dear reader, you know how I feel about free market economics. I honestly feel my views are both financially and metaphysically sound. Let me hasten to say, although I believe too many restrictions have recently been placed on our economy, I still think America is the land of great opportunity. Anyone can become very, very rich in this great land. I also believe that as a person decides to enjoy personal wealth, it is also beneficial that he become active to enhance and uphold a system that makes personal wealth so easily obtainable.

THE MYTH OF MONEY

The real truth about money is that it is a myth. It has no real value in and of itself. It is a medium of exchange. A one hundred dollar bill appears to be a real thing in and by itself, but it most certainly is not. A slice of bread has some value in itself; a hundred dollar bill, or several thousand one hundred dollar bills, does not. The best use one could get out of a million dollars worth of paper money, in and of itself, is perhaps a nice warm fire that would last for a short period of time.

Only through human agreement, as a medium of exchange for services and goods, does money assume value. It is what's behind the money that gives value to the money. Since any kind of wealth is nothing more than form manifested, the creation of all wealth and the medium used to express it begins in Mind. Out of no-thing comes everything. This is a fact about all objects in the physical world. Paper money is more easily understood when one realizes just what wealth really is.

Real wealth belongs to nature. The soil, rocks, water and earth yield true wealth. Paper money, checks and other documents merely serve as a convenient method to keep track of who is using nature's (God's) abundance.

MONEY AS A SYMBOL

In addition to being a medium of exchange, money is also a symbol—a symbol of wealth, freedom and self-expression. As an exchange vehicle, money is used for our convenience. As a symbol, it represents power, affluence and independence. As both a medium and symbol, it has no will or direction built within itself. It can only be used through self-direction. The power is not within it. The true power is in its creator.

Too often people make money their god. Money only represents prosperity. True prosperity is first a mental attitude. It symbolizes the prosperity consciousness. To apply right thinking and action to money we must recognize it for what it is—an outward expression of inner riches. The Bible tells us to keep our priorities in mind: "Seek ye first the Kingdom of God and his righteousness and all things shall be added unto you." (Matthew 6:33) A simplified explanation would be: Money is an effect, not a source. Put your attention on the source from which comes all outward forms and symbols of prosperity.

DO YOU DESERVE TO BE RICH?

How do you feel about that question? If you don't believe you deserve to be rich, you probably won't be, and if you do eventually have money, you won't fully enjoy it.

Once a person has decided that he wants to be rich, there are only two immediate obstacles in his path. His belief system faces only these two questions:

1. Do I deserve to be rich?
2. Do I believe I can be rich?

A positive "yes" answer (with feeling behind the word) to these two questions can lead you to unlimited wealth and prosperity. If you believe you deserve wealth and you believe you can be rich, it will be almost impossible for you not to accumulate huge sums of beautiful money and other forms of abundance.

POVERTY IS A STATE OF MIND

Poverty consciousness is the result of low self-esteem and negative thinking, nothing more and nothing less. A mental belief that upholds poverty consciousness is a learned condition. It is the result of what others have told you about or your feelings about money when you did not have any money. Your positive feelings about money have always been when you had a flow of money circulation in your life. Negative programming puts our attention on scarcity, restrictions and financial dissatisfaction. Thoughts centered on lack and limitation cause poverty consciousness and maintain it. Until prosperity consciousness prevails over poverty consciousness, the unnatural condition will linger and sabotage any efforts to reach financial freedom.

GET YOUR BIG "BUT" OUT OF THE WAY

"I would have been successful BUT—" is the big copout of people who did not quite make it. Here are a list of leading big Buts:

BUT I didn't have enough education
BUT the economy was bad
BUT I wasn't given a break
BUT I was unlucky
BUT I got married too young
BUT I had to support my family
BUT my divorce set me back
BUT my boss is a jerk
BUT they were jealous of me
BUT my parents were poor

If this list has not caught your BIG BUT, fill it in here:

I _____ would/could be successful

BUT: _____

Now, to win big success, just get your BIG BUT out of the way. It stands between you and achieving Total Success.

You need a reason to win or a reason to fail. Nobody becomes a loser without one or more (usually several) ifs, buts, would'as, should'as or could'as. To embrace success, you must let them go. You can have them or you can have success. You can't have both!

PROSPERITY CONSCIOUSNESS

Prosperity consciousness is a positive belief system—nothing more and nothing less. Your mind has two major functions: conscious (objective) and subconscious (subjective). Although separate in their reaction to stimuli and data, they are not divided or in opposition to each other. At any given moment your mind can act upon only one primary belief. When you send two ideas and feelings that are opposite in nature, your mind only will act upon the dominant one.

Example:

Ann works as a paralegal for a successful attorney. She desires a substantial raise in salary and feels she deserves it. She decides to approach her boss for a raise, and these are her thoughts as she prepares to ask him for a healthy raise. *I perform a vital service here at the office. I am deserving of a big raise. I have every right to be paid more money. I don't think he will give me what I deserve!*

Ann is sending two messages: one centered around her desire and belief in her deserving more money; the other core belief that it will not be granted. Only one will dominate. The dominant belief here appears to be "it won't happen." Thus, it is unlikely that it will, unless her boss has already decided to reward Ann with more money.

The completely positive mental approach would have gone like this: *I, Ann, deserve more money. I am a conscientious employee and I do excellent work. My boss values my valuable contribution and is pleased to give me a big salary increase. And so it is!* Now, that's a success affirmation with only one true message being sent. Chances are that the results will be favorable. In truth, chance has little to do with it!

Prosperity consciousness is centered upon the abundance that is found everywhere in this universe. Thoughts of lack and limitation are dismissed as soon as they "knock at the door" of the mind of the RICH-THINKER. The person who develops the prosperity consciousness will never again be poor. Even if he or she gets involved in an unprofitable venture, it will not take long to bounce back to riches. The late Mike Todd, the multimillionaire businessman and movie producer, summed up his wealth consciousness very nicely when he said, "I've never been poor, only broke. Being poor is a frame of mind. Being broke is only a temporary situation."

MONEY DOESN'T GROW ON TREES—
IT GROWS INSIDE YOUR HEAD

The source of all wealth, like everything else, is Mind. We have been conditioned by well-intended but nevertheless false programming. Parents, relatives and friends would have us accept the fact that money is a difficult commodity to get or keep. "Money doesn't grow on trees," is a popular slogan I heard every time I asked my mother for some change to satisfy my overactive sweet tooth in my youth. I can remember those innocent days very well. Living in a rural area outside St. Paul, Minnesota, it was a long walk, but one filled with anticipation, to go to the little combination grocery store/tavern named "Vera & Val's." It always amazed me how a handful of cold, hard, useless (to me) pennies, nickles and dimes could be exchanged for chocolate ice cream, Butter Finger candy bars, spearmint gum and assorted soda pop. In those days, I always felt I gave so little and received so much!

But soon I became conditioned, as most people are, how scarce those coins are. It took me a long time to realize that money is readily available and not at all scarce. There are dozens of things I like to do (write books, sell books, conduct workshops, act, help others sell merchandise, etc.) that people are eager to pay me money for. I also became aware that money can be multiplied. Money loves to make money and increase itself.

Real estate investing, the stock market and rare book buying and selling are just a few methods I have used to make money with money. By elevating my prosperity consciousness, I never feel poor. Sometimes I don't demonstrate as much money as I am capable of, and some investments (owning race horses, for one) and some personal adjustments (like getting divorced) have occasionally left me almost broke, but never poor. I know money grows in my mind. I know, as long as I deal fairly with other people and maintain high integrity and healthy self-confidence, money and me will always enjoy a good relationship. I have an agreement with the universe. It provides me with everything I need, and in return, I circulate abundance, benefitting others as I benefit. I strongly urge you to make a similar deal. It really works!

MONEY IS NOT THE CURE FOR POVERTY

Many people believe money solves poverty. It does seem logical: Give people what they don't have and the problem is solved, right? Wrong! No person's poverty consciousness was ever solved by giving him a handout. For many years the government has supervised dozens and dozens of poverty programs and given billions of dollars to the poor, with very little or no measurable results. You would think by now this wasteful practice would be stopped and a new effort at teaching prosperity consciousness would be instituted. But alas, today even more, money is being dumped into the bottomless pit. Poverty is such a big business today that hundreds of thousands of people earn their regular paycheck administering social and poverty programs. The programs do little to help the poor, but they do seem to help a lot of the paid "helpers", making the programs of at least some benefit. Treatment, to be successful, must be directed to Cause (Mind) and not to the poverty condition, which is an effect.

Prosperity thinking, never money, is the cure for poverty.

154

E. Joseph Cossman, who made millions in mail order, is fond of this wise saying: "Give a man a fish and you feed him for a day. Teach a man how to fish and you feed him for a lifetime."

MONEY HAS NOTHING TO DO
WITH HAPPINESS OR UNHAPPINESS

People seem to believe that money will make them happy or unhappy. Both premises are false. Even those who use the slogan "Money won't buy happiness," seldom really believe that basically true saying.

Rich has advantages over being poor for two reasons: (1) It allows you to get on with self-actualization in other areas of your experience and (2) it gives you the opportunity to get in touch with the fact that money doesn't create happiness. The poor person probably spends too much time and effort wrestling with money-related situations and wonders if money would bring total happiness. It won't, but tell that to someone lacking in prosperity and they will never believe you.

Money is fantastic, and it does offer more avenues to exciting new experiences (through travel, seminars, etc.), and when demonstrated in large sums, it will provide you with various adult-status toys (big homes, sleek cars, smart clothing, precious stones, ocean voyages, various collectibles, etc.) but never happiness. Happiness, too, is a state of mind, and while money can compliment and enhance it, it most certainly will not create it. The reverse is also true: Money can't make you unhappy, unless, of course, you decide to use it against yourself. And believe it or not, some people are masters at turning a potential blessing (money) into a curse.

155

THE MYTH OF MATERIALISM

Money and rich living are not unspiritual in any way. They are desirable and deserving conditions for all aware people.

Those who lack prosperity consciousness are usually the first to castigate those who are prosperous. They berate wealth and the wealthy and stress the importance of spirituality while they put down the materialistic. In so doing, they guarantee poverty consciousness will cling to them and hold them tightly in its grasp.

All forms of abundance, including money, are true spiritual conditions and are desirable and just for all human beings. Even those diehards who are fond of pointing to the Bible as justification to demean money seem to have misread scripture. The Bible does not state, as often is heard, that money is the root of all evil. The Bible clearly states, *"The love of money . . . "* My interpretation of this indicates pursuing money for money's sake and the hoarding of money can be degrading to man's spirit. Using money correctly to provide "good things" for ourselves and others is always right action. The individual demonstrating abundance by manifesting wealth and circulating money is living in alliance with Universal Law, assuming that he never invests or spends this precious substance for anything that is not in accord with positive living.

The entire physical word is materialized from the world of Mind. Wealth is a universal condition expressed by all that is. Money is not intrinsically good or evil. Your money can bless you daily or curse you continuously, depending on your interaction with it and your state of mind, which dictates your belief about it. Used for your highest expression, your money is God (good) in action.

LOVE AND WORK

"Work is love made visible."—Kahlil Gibran

Many people only turn their thoughts to joy, excitement and expression on the weekends. Monday through Friday are work days for most people and are often considered a time of stress and struggle. How sad it is that millions are unhappy in work activities that make up approximately one-third of their lives.

If your work seems dull, boring, self-limiting, or just a big hassle, there can only be two reasons:

1. You're not doing what you should do.
2. You're not doing what you want to.

Not doing what you should could mean that mental laziness or lack of commitment is preventing you from making a greater contribution to your present job or business. It could also indicate that you have not set high enough goals to hold your interest and spur you on to more productive contributions.

If you're not doing what you really want to do, who is stopping you? Only if your answer is "I am" are you telling it like it is. A human being must enjoy his labor in order to be truly fulfilled. Making money can be marvelous, and yet, working only to make money is most unsatisfying. If you dislike your work, money, even lots of it, will not bring fulfillment. In recent years both a popular family magazine and a highly respected psychological journal conducted surveys that found that between 25% and 33% of those interviewed "hated" their work. Overall, less than 28% stated they actually enjoyed their careers. Over 70% mildly or severely disliked or outright hated their work life.

To work at something you don't enjoy is to place yourself in a state of psychological bondage—a very low state of existence.

Deep in our Subconscious (also known as the "race mind") handed down from many generations, there are several antiquated beliefs that say work is a hardship, a curse upon humanity. This belief throughout the ages has proclaimed, "Man must live by the sweat of his brow," "Keep your nose to the grindstone," as well as many other grave and lifeless proclamations of work and woe. How can you help but feel tired, heavy and burdened by such "wisdom"? Only by facing the fact that this is a bunch of well-intended but nevertheless false mental garbage and then sweeping it out of your consciousness! The belief that it is natural to work long and hard, slowly killing yourself in order to "survive" is ridiculous. If your work isn't creative, fun, exciting and uplifting, as well as financially rewarding, change your attitude or change your job!

You were not meant to work forty hours a week so you can merely enjoy evenings, weekends, vacations or a secure retirement. If you love your life, you will also love your work. Before you change occupations, check out your attitude. If you're not in tune with a holistic approach to life, almost any kind of work will probably seem unpleasant to you.

You may find joy and meaning in your present work if you're willing to approach your occupation as an adventure rather than a necessary evil. When you love your work, your work will bring you great joy and satisfaction. When you love your work, the fruits of your labor, whatever type of work you do, will be a magnificent testimonial to your integrity and love.

FLO SHOWS US THE RIGHT ATTITUDE
TOWARD WORK

Florence K. could tell us all a lot about how the right attitude toward work can build prosperity. When her eleven and a half year marriage ended recently, Flo found herself in what appeared to be a tight spot. She had two young children and herself to support, and she had not been in the job market for several years, and even then, waitress work was all that she was familiar with. The trouble with that was she had never earned very much money in the past, considered herself only mediocre as a waitress and now needed lots more money. What to do?

For starters she enrolled in a new prosperity workshop offered by her local church. Using the beautiful and powerful "Millionaires of the Bible" prosperity books written by Catherine Ponder and published by DeVorss and Company, as guides, Flo became excited about her potential. She would apply for work at all of the leading San Diego area restaurants and supper clubs. She would use enthusiasm, goals and other success principles to be "the most prosperous waitress in town." She released all her past negative attitudes concerning waitress work (this work is demeaning for women; a lady has to put up with unruly customers; the pay is not good, etc.). Instead, she decided to make it go and make it Flo! And she did!!

Without effort, she found an attractive spot in which to serve the dining public. Flo applied the metaphysical prosperity principles she had learned and began earning a weekly income in excess of three times the ordinary waitresses income. So successful was Flo that she actually had to leave that restaurant to find a new and better job at another. This came about when her poverty-conscious fellow workers became envious of her smashing success. Four other waitresses who worked with her resented the fact that Flo was earning more tips than these other four coworkers combined. When these four ladies convinced management that all tips should be put into one pool and then distributed equally to all five waitresses at closing time, Flo took her stand. "I won't work under such conditions where a big lid is put on top of my earning power." The result: She found a better job at a better dining establishment and was assured whatever she earned was her own.

Florence K's story is a tribute to the "Can-Do" positive attitude. It also clearly illustrates how negative "can't-compete" people may become envious of one who is moving forward. Always seek the attitude that praises success and works to emulate it. If you let envy motivate you to try to bring down a successful person, you will only sabotage your own good. The "best" among us (those who always strive for excellence) always uplift us all. To clip the wings of an Eagle is to sin against ourselves and Nature.

Florence K. explained another success attitude to her close friends. "My desire to provide for the kids and myself gave

160

me plenty of motivation to make money; however, once I learned that friendliness and service were the main ingredients in serving diners, my love for my work and the money I received from it grew by leaps and bounds. At first I had to practice being attentive and cheerful, and this did pay off. When it became a sincere part of my personality, things got even better—a whole lot better!"

Not one to sit on her laurels, Flo has a new goal: to own her own fine restaurant within five years. With her kind of winning attitude, I wouldn't want to bet against it happening!

OF MEN AND MACHINES

Whatever we do, be it in sales and marketing, the arts or sciences, manufacturing, distribution, farming or education, if we do our task to benefit others spiritually, mentally or physically, we do perform a valuable service.

Today, machines are replacing people in many assembly-line jobs. At first workers and organized labor screamed and lobbied against these mechanical helpmates. Now, a New Age attitude is becoming more prevalent. Robots are a blessing. They can and will perform many of the mundane duties man has seldom felt full satisfaction in performing. The computer-operated machines will help increase productivity and open new horizons and new occupations for mankind. There is a "natural" inclination (subconscious conditioning) for humans to resist change. Most change (not all) ultimately improves the human condition.

A human is not a machine and is not meant to be treated like one. Whatever our work-related activities, most of us require new challenges, new stimuli and just compensation for work well done in order to make our work lives creative, productive, meaningful and joyous. If your work is not creative, productive, meaningful and joyous, you need to change occupations or change your attitude, or do both.

MIND OVER DESTINY

Some have adopted a fatalistic attitude about success as it relates to wealth-building. They may feel that they once had a great "chance" and blew it. They may now feel captive. To quote Shakespeare:

There is a tide in the affairs of men
Which taken at the flood leads on to fortune;
Omitted, all the voyage of their life
Is bound in shallows and in miseries.

This author knows there are "tides" in our lives that, like a mighty river, can move us quickly in its flow, and it may be said that life is somewhat cyclical. However, Mind is the absolute Law. When we tune into Universal Knowledge and successfully program our own subconscious correctly, this transcends all other outside influences.

You are already rich beyond your greatest dreams. Tap the motherlode of inborn riches and you will find yourself on a golden yacht, surrounded by a sea of prosperity.

CHANGING CAREERS

Change is something we usually want to avoid. While almost any career, business or job can be made interesting and become profitable, some are more suited for us because of our unique personalities and temperaments.

Human beings fight change, even changes that offer rich rewards and greater expression. Only by confronting our fears associated with making changes in our lives can we have any success in overcoming them.

Let's face it . . . making a career change, especially if you are well-established in your present career, is a major decision. Some anxiety is quite natural. After all, you may not be happy in what you are now doing, but you probably have security, and most of us like to cling to that.

Career changes do require taking risks. What I have learned about risks is—nothing really worthwhile happens until you take one. Happiness, love, wealth, all require taking some risks. If you have faith, if you really believe that God (all good) is with you and have plenty of healthy self-esteem, why not go for it? What have you really got to lose? Only something that you don't want anyway! The whole world and everything worthwhile in it belongs to the people who dare to be, do and have what they want to be, do and have. Prosperity consciousness means that you believe in yourself and your ability to make your life an adventure. Sometimes you will make a wrong choice. You may even scare yourself right out of your security blanket! Good!! If you ever do this, who or what will ever again be able to stop you?

If you are currently satisfied with your present occupation, you should be pleased. Just to test how tightly you are clutching your security blanket, consider what you would do if you were forced to make a career change. We live in a constantly changing world where the only true security comes from within, not in other people, things or occupations. Many businesses that employ thousands of people today will be obsolete a few years from now. Don't allow yourself to plant your feet or your mind in cement. Trust yourself and the new powers you are now developing. Realize where your job or your business came from, and know you can create another every bit as good, EVEN BETTER, any time you wish to.

WEALTH: A WISE MAN'S SERVANT

Money is truly a miser's master and a wise man's servant. To hoard wealth, always keeping it in an inactive state, is contrary to the law of multiplication and increase. Your wealth is to be used to elevate your consciousness and those in association with you. Universal Law always uses the sow and reap principle. This principle is very simple and very exact: Plant the seed, care for, cultivate and water it, and you will be rewarded with a bountiful harvest. For every single seed you put in the soil, you can receive thousands of new seeds, plus the fruit, all from the one.

Wealth multiplication works the precise same way. Money, when handled properly, will multiply and increase. The potent seed to a life of riches is inherent in every woman and man and only awaits "fertile soil," made ready by belief, to expand and increase.

Get enthusiastically involved in goal-setting, using the methods and techniques presented in Chapter Six. Soon you will be the master and steward of ever-increasing wealth. Money makes a very helpful servant or a very fearful master.

SPEAK OUT FOR PROSPERITY

With more and more people studying the positive thinking, holistic living and mental science approach to abundant living, "affirmations" are becoming extremely popular. Affirmations are not to be confused with traditional prayer; rather, they are a form of mental commands that invoke the Mind to act upon the good that is sought.

Affirmations can be silent or verbal. The word "affirm" means "to make firm." By repeatedly declaring the good (goals) you desire, rather than talking about what you lack, your subconscious can pick up your clear intent and begin acting upon it. Never underestimate the creative power of your words. You create your own world with your words (verbally as well as with the silent words of thought), as did Jehovah in the very beginning. If you are not pleased with the circumstances and conditions that you find in your present experience, be aware that you can change them by speaking new words of positive living.

Affirm your good now! Just make certain your word treatment is correctly phrased. Never affirm the negative. Don't say, "I don't have this and I need it." Instead, affirm: "This is what I want and I know it is mine." Giving thanks for something you don't already have but believe will be yours is a powerful mind-power demonstration. Faith, backed by the thankful heart, will not go unrewarded.

The six steps of a Scientific Mind Affirmation are:

1. BELIEVE that there is a Force that acts upon your words.

2. UNIFY with this Force and know it is ready to work for your good.

3. SPEAK YOUR WORD—Claim the good you desire. Be specific about for whom and what you treat.

4. ACCEPT—deny any false condition and affirm the truth.

5. GIVE THANKS—feel joy in knowing you have the Power working for you, with you and through you.

6. RELEASE IT—let go and let God.

All Truth-teachers and students who work with spiritual or scientific prayer or affirmations use the above six-step program. Some may speak their word (claim) in the first step and follow with belief and unifications. I have found it personally beneficial to affirm my belief and unify with my Source before making my claim. Use either sequence as you feel led. The bottom line is that this six-step program, effectively used, will put miracles into your experience.

Once you practice the steps of a Scientific Mind Affirmation and truly believe in this Power to bring you to your desires or your desire to you, it will become an extremely effective tool to use daily for your Total Success.

166

Bless and give thanks for who you are and what is now yours, and use daily affirmation treatments to bring more benefits and more abundance into your experience. Affirmations work wonders for increasing wealth, building better relationships, maintaining or restoring health, attracting love and for all other desired conditions and good things. They should be an integral part of your personal positive mind programming strategy for success.

THE LAW OF ABUNDANCE

All people in love with life and who practice prosperity thinking seek more abundance. They affirm increases in both quantity and quality in food, clothing, transportation, housing, knowledge, health, luxury, leisure, peace and satisfaction. These are not selfish, egotistical desires but normal, positive goals for anyone who is aware of the laws of abundance. How beautiful to live in accord with our true nature and use the miraculous law of abundance rather than to succumb to the false prophet that is lack and limitation and decreased expression.

The law of abundance always promotes expansion. There is a Universal Law for increase. There is no such law that upholds decrease. Abundance is what the Universe is all about, and to experience it in our life we need only unite with this Truth. Lack and limitation are foreign and unknown effects to the Principle of Life; nevertheless, as creative beings with free choice, we can experience them as an individualized expression if we so choose. This choice, of course, can be (and usually is) subjective and not objective.

Abundance is real and it is truth in the Universal sense.

167

Limitation is not recognized in the Universal sense. It is a false condition, yet we can give it undeserved power if we transfer our energy to it. In effect, we can make it our truth.

Here's an illustration about what is universally true and what is true for the person.

The earth has always been round. That's the way it is and always has been and always will be. Just five hundred years ago, most people did not believe the world was round. Almost everyone then believed the world was flat. So in effect their lives and activities were governed by this belief. Although universally erroneous, the belief did assume power in their lives. They made it their truth, and their mode of transportation, especially by sea, was governed by their belief.

The truth is always the truth and can never be other than the truth. At the same time, the individual may uphold a false notion and allow it to be "true" in his or her life. In so doing, a person can allow himself to be governed by a false premise and live at its effect. We become what we think we are!

Man is not a machine. Freedom of choice allows us to align ourselves with That Which Is or to live at the effect of something that isn't truthful, harmonious or life-expanding. The choice is ours. Just remember—the truth about your life is that you deserve only the best of everything, complete, unlimited abundance. To live in poverty you must convince yourself that lack and limitation is the way things are. If you convince yourself that there "isn't enough," you will soon be lacking things that you desire, and you will most certainly be limited. Outward appearances (abundance or lack) must always be the reflection of what you believe to be so.

AVOID TOUGH TIMES TALK

To reach abundant wealth and total financial freedom, only think, talk and act prosperous. When others tell you about impending "bad times" or how "the economy is in bad shape," do not align yourself mentally with such tales of woe. Likewise, don't buy into the sea of negativity available from television and radio news programs or your local newspaper. Anything opposed to rich thinking must not be allowed space in your conscious or subconscious. I am not telling you not to listen to what's happening in the financial world, positive and negative. I am saying that you should not "buy into" the negative.

You may have heard the story about the hamburger shop owner. Joe sold the biggest and best hamburger in town from a busy downtown corner location. Business was so good, Joe sent his son, Joe, Jr., to college to learn business and marketing. After four years in a leading institution of higher learning, Joe, Jr. returned. His father greeted him. "Great to have you back, Son. Business is better than ever. Now, I want to expand the business, rent the spot next door, knock down the dividing wall and really cash in big."

"Wait, Dad," Joe Jr. says. "Don't you know we are in the middle of a terrible recession? Times are tough. What we have to do is cut back. We'll reduce the size of our hamburgers twenty percent, stop giving away all these condiments and close earlier!"

Joe Sr. shook his head in disbelief, but decided his educated son must know what to expect from the economy. Soon business fell by nearly fifty percent, and old Joe sadly

169

had to admit to his son, "You were right, Joey, times really *are* tough."

Good, bad, terrific or tough, it is all really a state of mind. Human beings have too often developed a perverted "love affair" with bad news. The front page of your daily paper is filled with stories of murder, rape, robbery, wars, threats of wars and impending disasters—all in big black headlines. In small print on page twenty-three, if you're lucky, you might read something about man's positive achievements or an inspiring story about love or human kindness. Do you still wonder why mankind appears to be in less than a desirable state?

What you think of and talk about, you will act upon. For the sake of your prosperity, avoid "tough times" talk.

DIRECT YOUR MONEY FLOW WITH GOALS

Although I have already presented a whole chapter on goal-setting and goal-achieving, I think it would be wise here to reiterate: Goals can lead you up the stairway to Total Success. In the exciting arena of wealth-building, they are indispensable to be rich in record time. You should set daily goals and weekly goals, along with long-range big goals. Always remember—once money begins to materialize and circulate in your life, you must self-direct it for best results, forever increasing the flow. Become a "money magnet" by using self-direction and goals. Once you have begun to create more prosperity in your experience, it is time to direct and increase the money flow with the wealth strategy of the very, very rich—wealth pyramiding.

WEALTH PYRAMIDING

The richest people in the world all make use of wealth-pyramiding, and so can you. The strategy behind wealth pyramiding, or as I love to call it, "money making money," is simple. Money is used to multiply itself. You may own a profitable business or hold a high-paying job. Your business or job can provide you with all of the necessities and some of the luxuries of life. Real wealth, however, is only obtainable by putting your money to work for you, making more money. Look over the following example of wealth pyramiding in action.

TAKE YOUR CHOICE

You are given two employment offers. Both will last only one month and one week, a total of 37 days!

Your first offer will bring you one thousand dollars ($1,000) a day for 37 days.

Your second offer is one cent (1¢) the first day and double that amount each day until the 37 days are up.

Here are the results:

DAY	OFFER #1 DOLLARS	OFFER #2 DOLLARS
1	$ 1,000	$ .01
2	1,000	.02
3	1,000	.04
4	1,000	.08
5	1,000	.16
6	1,000	.32
7	1,000	.64
8	1,000	1.28
9	1,000	2.55
10	1,000	5.10
11	1,000	10.20
12	1,000	20.40
13	1,000	40.80
14	1,000	81.60
15	1,000	163.20
16	1,000	326.40
17	1,000	650.00
18	1,000	1,300.00
19	1,000	2,600.00
20	1,000	5,200.00
21	1,000	10,400.00
22	1,000	20,800.00
23	1,000	41,600.00
24	1,000	83,200.00
25	1,000	165,750.00
26	1,000	331,500.00
27	1,000	663,000.00
28	1,000	1,326,000.00
29	1,000	2,652,000.00
30	1,000	5,304,000.00
31	1,000	10,608,000.00
32	1,000	21,216,000.00
33	1,000	42,432,000.00
34	1,000	84,864,000.00
35	1,000	169,728,000.00
36	1,000	339,456,000.00
37	1,000	678,912,000.00

Total $37,000   Total $678,912,000.00

Offer #1 would bring you a nice $37,000 for 37 days. Now, consider Offer #2—double-your-money pyramiding in just 37 days, starting with a lowly penny would yield you SIX HUNDRED AND SEVENTY-EIGHT MILLION, NINE HUNDRED AND TWELVE THOUSAND DOLLARS! A fabulous fortune!! Nearly six hundred and seventy-nine million in just 37 days may not seem realistic to you, but the concept of money making money is 100% valid!

Investing in real estate, oil drillings, precious metals or stones, or the stock market are just four methods to allow your money to make more money. Another traditional investment is putting money in the bank. However, interest from banks and other financial institutions is generally quite low and does not allow fast increase. Seek the investments that offer the largest return and still offer reasonable security.

More people have become millionaires investing in real estate than all other investments combined. Let's see how wealth pyramiding works with real estate investing.

ONE THOUSAND TO ONE MILLION
IN JUST TEN MULTIPLES

Starting with one thousand dollars, just ten multiples can make a millionaire out of the astute real estate investor, if she or he can double up on each investment.

STARTING CAPITAL: One thousand dollars

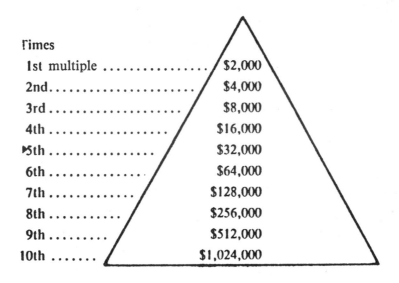

Times
1st multiple $2,000
2nd..................... $4,000
3rd.................... $8,000
4th................. $16,000
5th $32,000
6th $64,000
7th $128,000
8th $256,000
9th $512,000
10th $1,024,000

One million and twenty-four thousand dollars is the yield from the tenth multiple.

While examples presented here are just that, never underestimate the wealth-building power of Wealth Pyramiding. A profitable business or good job can provide you with a large measure of abundant living, and that's all some of us desire. If you desire much more, and you have every right to want more, then you should realize that you must make your money continuously earn you more money. Your money will multiply faster than rabbits when you put money multiplication to work—24 hours a day—for you!

174

Even if you do not desire millions, you still will greatly benefit and enjoy more rich-living by making your money work for your good. The Law of Increase is in perfect harmony with this principle.

THE LAW OF INCREASE

The Universe is forever expanding and creating more, and this fact also can apply to your prosperity.

Life is cyclical, full of peaks and valleys, but overall movement is always forward. The Law of Increase, as it applies to money-making, states that things will always get better and increase in value—good stocks and bonds, precious metals, real estate, etc.—they will always go up in value and be substantially higher five years from now than they are today.

Making, saving and investing money should be a routine in our lives without a do-or-die urgency to it. It is not conducive to prosperity living to procrastinate or refrain from making decisions. At the same time, it is not wise to rush into things or attempt to accomplish everything at once. Use your business or job as your source of day-to-day living, and use your investments to increase your overall wealth. Above all, never forget that the real riches *are inside your mind!*

THE LAZY WAY TO WEALTH

Most people have been taught to loathe laziness and to consider it an evil condition. Quite the contrary, I've found that a healthy mental attitude about laziness is a helpful tool in becoming prosperous.

We live in a society caught up in a whirlwind of frenzied activities, unnatural competition and unnecessary strife. The result: high anxiety and increased stress. People are confronted with so much turmoil that many long for old age and retirement as an exit from what they perceive as "dog-eat-dog" living. We want to get off the roller coaster, kick back and relax. And we should! You deserve to take time off. It's a good idea to take a day now and then where you simply loaf. The person who feels he is on a treadmill but cannot get off for even a little relaxation because "if I don't keep at it constantly, it will all fall apart" is a person imbedded in poverty consciousness.

Human beings are not machines. We need regular time off to loaf, relax and reflect. I used to take one long vacation (three or four weeks) once per year, with little or no time off in between. Recently, I have discovered this does not work nearly as well as several "short vacations" on a semi-regular basis. A three or four day trip to the desert or mountains is a marvelous getaway. I am refreshed, invigorated, anxious and happy to return to my writings. More importantly, my craft improves as my mind is filled with many stimulating new ideas as a result of each short getaway.

In my discussions and interviews with very productive individuals, real achievers from the world of business, entertainment, the arts and sports, I have discovered most of these creative people also are greatly stimulated and revitalized by taking a little time off. Such time off is not wasted but prepares one to achieve even more. Even when a person does not outwardly dwell on new ideas or solutions related to his business, the mind is still being recharged and great new ideas begin to forge to the surface.

176

You may be taking time off to relax and loaf and do very little physically, but your mind is never inactive. Your creative thinking process can never be turned off. In effect, by relaxing and clearing your body and mind, you make room for Creative Intelligence to give you new success signals. Laziness for the "walking-dead" (the person without belief, faith, self-esteem or any self-directed goals) can be a negative way of life, while occasional laziness for the person with purpose in his life is a time to recharge spiritually, mentally and physically. It is in this period of little or no outer-activity that great creative insights may be received. In the hustle and bustle of daily living, too often we do not quiet our mind and relax our body long enough to receive the creative signals that we are always being sent. Even the person who prays and/or meditates daily still needs additional time off to rejuvenate the body and enrich the brain.

Time off to be lazy after you have reached some major goal or accomplished a worthwhile task is a super way to reward yourself. As a byproduct of this "earned time off for laziness," you will be amazed at the bright ideas you will receive for new projects and goals during periods of limited physical activity.

For the sake of good health alone, you must give yourself regular time off to relax. The words of my friend, Kay B., ring in my ears. Her husband, Ben, was a hard-driving corporate executive who rarely took time off and who worked 55-65 hours a week. In spite of pleas from family, friends and his doctor, Ben refused to take time off to relax. Kay told me, "Ben's favorite retort when asked to take a little time to enjoy life outside of work was, 'I don't have the time to take time off. There will be plenty of time to relax when I retire.' " Ben was too busy to take time off, but unfortunately not too busy to die before reaching his retirement. This tragic example should serve to remind us all how important it is to give ourselves time to do nothing but relax. You may have been erroneously told all forms of laziness are bad or even sinful. Don't allow guilt from parental or society hangups to keep yourself from enjoying a degree of laziness. Occasional periods of laziness are very good for you.

WAKE UP THE SLEEPING GENIUS
INSIDE OF YOU

In addition to being able to observe and perceive, everyone possesses deeper mind power abilities of intuition followed by creative imagination and dreaming, telepathy, clairvoyance, precognition, etc. These marvelous powers of the Inner Mind will be discussed in detail in Chapter 12, and are mentioned here only because they work so well to bring more wealth into our experience.

The basic idea behind the creation of wealth is this: You can't be rich in your pocketbook until you're rich in your mind. Mind is the creator of all that is in the physical world. In dealing with this unlimited power that is Mind, it behooves us to sharpen and use every mental tool at our disposal.

Intuition is a powerful mental tool to use in attracting riches. It may be a good idea to point out here and now, this author does not believe one gets rich, although this is a common way to state it, but rather that one attracts wealth through becoming rich on the mental level. Real wealth is always within.

Intuition is a spiritual (abstract) mental faculty of a human being's mind that when fully developed points out the best direction to take in our lives. Human reasoning may be a helpful, brain-oriented faculty, but it is not as potent an inner-sensitivity power as is intuition.

Intuition counsels you with a "yes" or "no", a quiet "do it" or "don't do it" gentle feeling that prompts you from within. It never tries to convince you to do anything; it only responds in the stillness when you seek direction and turn within. If intuition does not seem to be active in your experience, it is only because you are not tuned in. It is a marvelous, discerning power available to us all. You can easily learn to contact and receive guidance by daily observing quiet times. When the mind is free of most of our thoughts, it is receptive to intuitive guidance. The silent time following a period of meditation is an excellent time to obtain intuitive answers. Intuition is a gentle prodder, and her ways are very subtle. People living only with and at the effect of life's outer conditions are usually unable to "feel" or "sense" this miraculous power or to heed its gentle but knowing guidance. It is always there sending signals, but we must tune in to pick up the silent messages.

To effectively gain wisdom from our intuition, we must first accept it as a real thing. Once we accept it as something we can use to make the right decision in our lives, we will be inclined to seek its counsel often.

Train yourself to "tune in" often when you need direction and questions answered. The more aware you become of this inner knowledge and its ability to give you precise guidance, the less mental stress and anxiety you will exert in wrestling with your problems. Soon you will be aware that the right answer to your questions concerning relationships, health, business or investments is readily available to you. This frees you from wasteful worry and effort. You will no longer have to try to control people, places or situations. You can stop maneuvering and manipulating. Through inner awareness, all answers are available. A never-ending supply of profitable ideas and methods or right action are ready to come forth and point the direction to even greater success.

Suddenly, you will "get a hunch" or "feel" as to which direction to take or what to do or what not to do. You will soon discover that as you follow your intuitive feelings, without becoming too analytic, your good will come to you quickly and without struggle. Even those goals you put on a realistic time table will become reality far sooner than expected. Next will come the major breakthroughs. Successful surprises will begin exploding in your life. Your goals will be achieved in record time and more good than you ever hoped for will rush into your experience. Intuition will be used without rationalization by you consciously, without hesitation, to open the flood gates and shower yourself with personal prosperity and all forms of rich living.

Once one has learned to consciously use the knowing power of intuition in his experience, other gifts of the mind (imagination, dreaming, telepathy, clairvoyance, etc.) will also be presented to be used as success guides and to raise a person's knowingness to new, elevated vibrations of higher consciousness and unrestricted expression.

THE TEN COMMANDMENTS OF PROSPERITY

To achieve total wealth and enjoy unlimited riches, many new attitudes concerning prosperity must be cultivated. These "Ten Commandments of Prosperity" will help you rid yourself of negative concepts that actually prevent you from living abundantly. It is only positive affirmations that will attract wealth to you. Try the following ten daily and expect positive results!

I. *THOU SHALT NOT THINK PROSPERITY IS EVIL.*
Rather, think and proclaim: "Prosperity is right and good for me, and I graciously accept it as proper and beneficial for me and others in my experience. I want and use ever-increasing wealth for good purposes. I thank God for my prosperity."

II. *THOU SHALT NOT SPEAK OR THINK NEGATIVELY ABOUT PROSPERITY.*
Do not say that "It is difficult to be prosperous" or that "It is hard to obtain enough money." Rather, think and proclaim: "I see myself surrounded with wealth. I see myself enjoying more and more beautiful, green money. I am deserving, open and receptive to greater abundance, and I use my ever-increasing wealth wisely."

III. *THOU SHALT NOT MISUSE THY PROSPERITY.*
All negative ideas about money originate from the premise that money/wealth is often made at the expense of others. Think and proclaim: I have the right attitude about money and prosperity. I do no wrong

with my wealth or no evil to obtain wealth. Right-thinking and right action draws ever-increasing prosperity to me like a magnet."

IV. *THOU SHALT SHARE THY PROSPERITY.*
Hoarding wealth is contrary to the Law of Abundance. You must give more so that you can receive more. Think and proclaim: "I give money to worthy causes that reflect my beliefs. I plant money seeds and I reap an ever-increasing prosperity harvest. I give with a joyful heart, knowing as I give I receive whatever I give back, multiplied many times over."

V. *THOU SHALT REMEMBER THY THOUGHTS ATTRACT THY PROSPERITY.*
Wealth is not something "out there" that you must try to get. Prosperity is a state of mind. Riches begin in Mind. Think and proclaim: "The Universe is abundantly prosperous and is anxious that I prosper. The more I use and enjoy wealth for good purposes, the more wealth is attracted to me to enrich my life. My mind, cooperating with Universal Intelligence, is my wealth source."

VI. *THOU SHALT NOT WORSHIP THY WEALTH.*
The Bible and other great spiritual books made it clear that great money and wealth prosperity are not enough to bring one joy, peace and true happiness. Think and proclaim: "Money is not my master; it is my obedient servant. I use my prosperity wisely and never allow it to use or manipulate me. I am never at the mercy of greed."

*VII. THOU SHALT LOVE THYSELF ENOUGH TO
REALIZE THAT THEE DESERVES UNLIMITED
PROSPERITY AND EVER-INCREASING ABUN-
DANCE.*

*Thoughts that you are undeserving of prosperity will
keep you deep in the quicksand of poverty consciousness. As a unique child of God, you deserve all good
things, and you deserve them abundantly! Think and
proclaim: "I Am that I Am. I love this life that is in
me. I am good, loving, creative and kind. I deserve
the best of everything, including ever-increasing prosperity, and I am becoming prosperous right now!*

*VIII. THOU SHALT NOT BE ENVIOUS OF OTHERS
WHO ARE PROSPEROUS.*

*A person with envy in his heart tends to think and
speak negatively about those who have possessions
that they desire but believe they lack. This attitude
is a huge roadblock to a prosperity consciousness.
Never put down the rich because they have great
wealth. Bless them for their wealth demonstration.
Think and proclaim: "I give thanks that so many
others are expressing so much beautiful prosperity in
their lives. I give thanks for all that I now have and all
that is being attracted to me, for I, too, am rich in
happiness, love, joy, health, self-expression and
creativity."*

IX. THOU SHALT PYRAMID THY PROSPERITY.

*Money making money is "prosperity acting upon
prosperity." This is the fastest way to increase your
wealth. Think and proclaim: "My money serves me
through wealth multiplication. My prosperity in-*

183

creases and expands. I see my money making more money. The law of increase is active in my life. More prosperity is always flooding into my experience. I thank God for the wealth-pyramid I am now building."

X. *THOU SHALT BUILD A POSITIVE CASH FLOW. Going into debt for anything but the best sound investments can lead to financial suicide. To enjoy great prosperity you must be a good steward with your wealth and not spend money that you do not have. With the possible exception of your home and your automobile, pay cash for the things you want. Going into debt can sabotage your prosperity consciousness. Think and proclaim: "I recreate and maintain a positive cash flow in my life. I pay cash for most things I want and always have enough cash to do so. I know I'll always have all the cash necessary for prosperous living, and I am very thankful this is true. And so it is."*

THE WEALTH-BUILDING POWER
OF A SUCCESS COVENANT

The writing down of success affirmations and wealth goals has benefitted many. A Success Covenant is a very unique, valuable technique that takes our written word into an even deeper level of Spiritual/Mind Treatment.

A Success Covenant must always be two-fold. Some degree of belief in God is necessary. A Success Covenant is a spiritual agreement. If you cannot come to terms with consciously entering into an agreement (covenant) with God, you should continue to visualize your success and write down your goals. If you feel comfortable by now with "Spiritual Stuff" (and I realize many readers were ardent believers before they ever picked up this book), I am going to present to you, perhaps, the most powerful spiritual success method any man or woman can use to claim unlimited abundance and all good things that are desired.

Although two-fold in nature, a Success Covenant is never "bargaining with God." You are not pleading for something. In using a covenant, you are giving as well as receiving.

In the Bible, the book of Genesis tells how Jacob entered into a Success Covenant with Jehovah that perfectly demonstrates the two-fold aspects of a Success Covenant.

Jacob had just been through a time of much trial and tribulation and was anxious to reunite with the healing and prospering power of his God. He desired blessing, prosperity, guidance and a complete reconciliation with his family. Here is the covenant he entered into:

"If God will be with me and keep me in the way that I go and will give me bread to eat and raiment to put on so that I come again to my father's house in peace, and Jehovah will be my God,

"Of all that thou shalt give me, I will surely give the tenth unto thee."

How often does a man or woman on bended knee ask for this or that blessing only to stop there? In going one big step further, by making an agreement on what we will do in return for a miracle or blessing, we form the Divine Covenant.

Jacob's Success Covenant worked perfectly. The agreement was honored on all sides, and Jacob returned to his father's home in peace, a very wealthy man. Jacob's Success Covenant was not merely a prayer about what he wanted from God. He did first ask for multiple blessings but then entered into a covenant by stating what he would do in return for the many favors he desired. Agreeing to give a tenth of all that he received solidified the important, two-fold nature of the covenant.

Never enter a covenant asking for anything but that which shall bless you and others, and never state you will do something in return unless you are completely committed to it. To enter into a Success Covenant with the Source of Everything and not fulfill your agreement is to invite failure. You can't cheat God and expect to win.

A Success Covenant requires that you must "vow a vow." This is a sacred spiritual act and is not to be taken lightly. Even today it is practiced throughout the Holy Land and the Middle East, and no person in that part of the world would think of not fulfilling his part of a sacred covenant. During Biblical times, to break a voluntary vow was to court punishment of death.

In this day of New Age enlightenment, we need not perceive God (Universal Knowledge) as vengeful or vindictive. Nevertheless, to demonstrate our faith correctly, it would be unwise to "vow a vow" unless we fully intended to keep our part of a covenant to the fullest degree.

In making a Success Covenant, you should be very specific about what you are asking for and what you will do in return. Writing it down will help clarify all aspects of your spiritual agreement. Giving a tenth (tithing) of the abundance you receive is a fairly common agreement made by those who enter into a Success Covenant. However, some agree to give more to spiritual work. Few who enter into this Divine Agreement would offer less. Occasionally a person will offer something else besides a portion of the good he or she receives. One man told me he asked for many, many blessings for himself and his family and kept his part of the covenant by becoming a minister. A woman recently shared with me that the blessings she wanted had nothing to do with wealth but rather the gifts of health and family harmony. In return, she gave one day a week, without pay, working to improve conditions for the elderly in her city.

You may offer any worthwhile activity instead of or in addition to giving back a portion of the prosperity or other benefits you seek. Since it is vital to the covenant that you fulfill your part of it, do not vow to do something that you don't fully intend to do, and never vow to do something that you really don't want to do. There should be only love and joy and a glad heart in completing your part of the spiritual agreement that makes a Success Covenant work!

Another important aspect of a Success Covenant is to immediately get busy fulfilling your part of the sacred agreement.

A singer named Tina was having career problems. (Problems in the sense that she was not working regularly and needed money badly.) She entered into a Success Covenant after reading books by Catherine Ponder and listening to cassette tapes by Rev. Ike—two leading prosperity teachers. She asked God for great success in her career and financial abundance as a result of her talent. In return, she would give a tenth of all money paid to her for singing engagements. A few days after entering into the covenant, her agent called to tell her she had been booked for two weeks in the lounge of a well-known West Coast hotel. Tina earned fifteen hundred dollars for this two-week gig. She immediately spent the fifteen hundred dollars to pay off some old bills and to buy herself two beautiful new outfits that would enhance her stage presence. She neglected to give a tenth, in this case $150, to her church as she had vowed she would when she made her Success Covenant.

When new singing assignments were not immediately offered to her, she realized she had broken her solemn vow. She meditated and prayed about her default. Weeks later, when everything looked bleak and she was about to abandon her singing career and seek employment in banking where she once worked as a teller, a one-week engagement at a popular Los Angeles club was offered to her, substituting for the lead singer, who was taking a week off to get married and honeymoon.

Upon being paid seven hundred dollars for the one-week assignment, Tina came to terms with her covenant. She gave $220 to her church, giving both a tenth of the second job's pay as well as a tenth of the first job's pay. With her Success Covenant reinstated and in complete balance, exciting new offers rushed to her. Soon she was able to be very selective about where she worked and who she worked for.

She now works regularly, as often as she wants to, at leading clubs and hotels throughout the west coast and commands contracts that offer her up to twelve hundred dollars weekly and never less than a thousand a week.

Does Tina still give a tenth of every dollar she earns singing? "You better believe I do," she recently told me. "I will never renege on my covenant again. The more willing I am to give, the more I receive. I don't want to ever change that."

Upon entering into a Success Covenant, it is important that you demonstrate your faith in the covenant by fulfilling your part of the agreement as soon as possible. Giving even before you receive is a grand demonstration of your belief that you can speed up desired results. You may have agreed to give a tenth of what you will receive, yet giving a portion of what you already have, even if your gift is small, will put your faith into action. A little "seed money" planted by you right after making a Success Covenant shows your good faith and can help you reap an abundant harvest.

A word of caution. Although I am very pleased to share the previous wealth-building power of Success Covenants with you, the reader, I don't want you to be misled. The Covenant I am talking about is with the Divine Spirit within, and NOT a judgmental God sitting on some cloud in the heavens. Every person is entitled to his own concept of God, but my Mental Science premise requires that I clearly state that I believe in the unity of God and man and all that is.

REJOICE AS YOU BECOME RICH

"Money, which represents the prose of life, and which is hardly spoken of in parlors without an apology, is, in its effects and laws, as beautiful as roses."
—Ralph Waldo Emerson

Creating wealth and making more money is fun. Wealth-building is a far more stimulating experience than inheriting a fortune. The true entrepreneur is alive and vibrant, a joy to behold, and an exciting personality to be around. The man or woman in the process of creating prosperity looks like, acts like and is a WINNER! By contrast, the sons and daughters of the very rich, who are spoon-fed abundance, often are a dull, dreary and boring lot. There are magnificent exceptions, such as the aware and stimulating daughter or son of a tycoon or the abrasive wealth-seekers whose tactics resemble the performance of a Mack truck. Overall, the wealth-creator, or for that matter, any person in the process of building and creating anything beneficial, is a source of magnetic power and towering inspiration. We love to be next to powerful, inspiring people, and well we should. All men and women are uplifted by the creative achievers in our midst. Thank God for the successful!

Free your mind of all thoughts of lack, limitation and "not enough" thinking. Realize you live in a universe of infinite abundance. Know that your success will uplift you and those nearest you. Know that money is a medium of exchange and an outward symbol of the Creative Force that is within. Read the "Ten Commandments of Prosperity" daily. Create wealth that will serve you well and then make your money make money. Use your money to enrich yourself and others.

If you are rich in Spirit, you will be rich in your mind. When you are rich in your mind, you will be prosperous. Then you will have what you want and you will want (and enjoy) what you have.

"Our physical and mental bodies are spiritually designed to be perfect, but are sometimes influenced and distorted by our false beliefs."

—BEING A CHRIST TEXTBOOK*
BY ANN P. MEYER AND PETER V. MEYER

*BEING A CHRIST, by Ann P. Meyer & Peter V. Meyer © 1975, Dawning Publications, San Diego, CA.

Chapter Nine

THE WHOLE MIND
APPROACH TO HEALTH

The two most exciting developments in the health care field are (1) the new holistic approach to health and (2) preventive health care. The one truth concerning optimum health is that your mind can make (keep) you well. While some in the medical profession still see disease as "something out there that could get you," increasing numbers of people, including a growing number of medical professionals, view the treatment and care of the body as unseparated from the person's mind and emotions.

Everything begins in mind, as Jack Ensign Addington points out in his dynamic and revealing book, *Psychogenesis*: "Mind plus beginning means everything begins in mind." Your every experience comes out of your mind, which is an individual extension of Universal Mind, which is All That Is.

By learning how to think healthy, you will learn how to live healthy. In dissecting the word "disease", we can discover the root of illness—dis-ease. Where there is absence or lack of harmony there will be fears and doubts, which in turn create stress. Prolonged stress invites physical and emotional problems.

A human being is a Spiritual/Mental entity that relates to outside stimuli through the use of a physical body. Our bodies are temples maintained by our minds. Our bodies are not passive; they can and do send us many signals as to what

Psychogenesis © 1971 by Jack Ensign Addington, Dodd, Mead & Co., NY, NY they desire (food, shelter, care, etc.), and built within the human organism is the miraculous ability to safeguard most of its functions and rejuvenate itself. Still, your mind is your body's master, for if the mind decides to risk life and limb in some heroic or dumb act, the body will be forced to go along with the deed. And when some poor soul, immersed in stress and deep depression, decides to hurl himself over the bridge, the "No! Don't do this!" signal from his body will not stop the suicidal act if the person's mind is on fire and his desire to "escape life" has taken control.

From the greatest inspirational act to the most hideous crime, everything begins in mind. At the Universal level, there is only Love and the Law. Wrong action, disease and other disorders are never the result of our true, loving, and harmonious nature. They arise out of perverted (misguided) application of the Law of Life, which then acts as a cosmic mirror. What is happening on the inside is reflected on the outside.

YOUR MIND'S DIET

Physical dieting has reached epidemic proportions in America. Millions of people are experimenting with hundreds of diets. The bestseller lists reflect the great popularity of almost anything written on the subject of losing weight or new approaches to nutrition. Professionals in the field of biochemistry have discovered most physical problems result from glandular deficiencies and psychological strife. Behind these problems are found the real culprit—mental disturbance—which creates mental imbalance.

Mind Science recognizes the valuable contributions made by the physician and the psychiatrist. Good doctors and others in the healing profession can help correct physical or mental disorders, but ultimately the individual is responsible for his own well-being.

Mental causation is invisible and usually emotional. The physician diagnoses the body and prescribes a remedy. The psychiatrist diagnoses a person's emotional state and also makes suggestions that may lead to better mental balance. Both perform valuable services, while at the same time usually treating the effect, not the problem. The metaphysician looks for change at the level of cause—Mind. The actual treatment of the cause behind the problem must be within man's mind. Everything begins in mind. Working with the physical body to correct distortions is the rightful province of medical men and women. We can be thankful that many medical people have recently been persuaded by New Thought to take a holistic approach to health and healing. Medical wonders are wrought when a medical man or woman acts against disease as both physician and metaphysician.

While we can be very thankful for great healings of humans by either medical, psychological or spiritual means, let us resolve to prevent problems from manifesting through correct living patterns.

Love is the best safeguard against emotional and physical problems. Lack of love and harmony creates an atmosphere of stress and tension. This is the breeding ground of all sorts of physical, mental and emotional havoc.

To control weight or to work with sound nutritional principles is admirable and can pay welcome dividends. A sound mental diet is of paramount importance to the person who desires optimum living. Excessive amounts of sugar, salt, alcohol, drugs and fats are contrary to positive health. Any amount of thought on lack, limitation, resentment and envy is the enemy of a sound mental diet. Love is the greatest health tonic for harmony and self-satisfaction. Joy and all other good vibrations are always in its healing wake.

Show me a person who loves life and everything in it and harbors no resentments, and I'll show you a person who lives with joy and harmony and incredible power. Love forms an impregnable shield against all forms of disorder.

Hence, the person who prescribes for himself a mental diet centered around love surrounds himself with the Universe's most powerful antibiotic and vaccination. Disease is foreign to this elevated state of consciousness.

ARE YOU LIVING OR JUST ALIVE?

There is a difference. Over twenty years ago I worked as a recreational therapist and psychiatric technician at a major mental hospital in the Midwest. Although most employees at this institution were doing their best to provide good patient care, many of the practices of the sixties are already antiquated by today's improved standards. Far too few doctors, nurses, therapists, technicians and aides were employed for the large patient population. Also, electric shock treatment was, in my opinion, excessively used as a potential cure for a cornucopia of mental disorders. Conditions at that institution were far less than ideal during the sixties. Nevertheless,

196

they were very modern and humane when compared to conditions that existed prior to World War II. Prior to World War II, mental illness was not a subject to be discussed in "polite society," and the mentally disturbed were often treated with less kindness than were most animals.

As a remnant of the dark ages of mental health, a handful of long-term, permanent patients from those days were found on the institution's "maintenance wards"—all victims of man's great misuse of the surgical knife on the brain of his fellow man. To look into the eyes of a lobotomized person is to stare into a vacuum. The person can move, eat and may even babble a few words, but when you look into his eyes, you know there is nobody home.

I believe in life after life and in love and renewal. Knowing this, I know that everyone created in the image and likeness of the All-Knowing One will eventually find peace and great new expression. And still, what a sobering effect it is to look into another's eyes and see no one there. Sadly, the very same vacancy I noticed many years ago in the eyes of some individuals at the mental hospital are evident today in many people in every-day society. I will concede that they may be functioning better. They may cook their own meals, raise kids, hold a job and/or travel about. At the same time that they appear to be relating to their environment, their eyes and their expression tell another tale. It appears many human beings have put their mental and emotional living responses on "hold" and are operating on "automatic pilot" to "walk through" their daily duties which they may dread but know they must perform.

The person who gives up on himself and relinquishes his zest for living may remain alive, but the life force will not be vividly expressive. It may not even be evident. All is consciousness and consciousness is what we are. To give up our sensitivity, our curiosity and our awareness is to camouflage the lifespring within us. Increased sensitivity and curiosity allows us to be more aware of our body. Stress tears down the door to our resistance—not in one fell swoop, but through a subtle process—much the same way termites attack a succulent piece of wood.

Awareness of our emotional and physical "signal system" allows us to handle stress with new positive responses. In so doing, the life force inside advances and expands. Heaven or hell, you must decide. You can either perceive life as an endless struggle in which we "are overcome by hardships" or the magnificent experience in which we may offer this joyous praise: *"I am overwhelmed by the beauty I see in everything. Thank you, wonderful God."*

THE HIGH COST OF HEALTH CARE

Dr. Jonathon Miller, a health care professional in New York, recently remarked, "People have become alienated by astronomical health care costs. With the possible exception of the public utilities, we are the most mistrusted of the vital services."

Traditional health care in America, which includes medical insurance, is currently the third largest industry in the nation. Medical costs have risen to nearly ten percent of our Gross National Product. Costs have definitely skyrocketed, greatly outpacing general inflation. Costs have eclipsed the means of average people, apparently giving the heavily insured and the very rich advantages in health care.

While making a lot of money is a very worthwhile activity that this author greatly encourages, I sincerely believe there are millions of ways to circulate it far superior to spending it on disease-related expenses. I'm reminded of the colorful old (but highly unmetaphysical) Yiddish curse: "May you make a million dollars and spend it all on doctor bills!" Correct thinking dictates that we never wish such a fate upon anyone, nor experience it ourselves.

While traditional medicine continues to advance and does much good, like most bloated establishment entities, waste, neglect and unwillingness to change have been built within the system. One of the most severe and disturbing medical problems today is inatrogenic illness. Inatrogenic means "doctor-caused" illness. The unfavorable effects of hospitalization, surgical complications or surgical mistakes, the side effects of drugs or prescribing the wrong medicine are among the most common doctor-caused problems.

The burdens of medical practice have taken their toll on our doctors. A recent national poll disclosed 44 percent of the public does not believe physicians are "ethical or honest." Professional organization surveys estimate that approximately ten percent of all physicians are seriously addicted to drugs or alcohol. Physicians are more likely than any other professional group to experience mental disorders, commit suicide or be sued. Talk about stress! The men and women of the medical profession know the word well! As the patient cries out against insensitivity and problems of dehumanization, the medical professional faces the very same problems.

An overview into established medical practices with all its related problems clearly indicates the emphasis is still far too

199

heavily involved with wrestling with the effect (the manifested disease/disorder) with not enough attention given to cause—what's happening in the mind! The belief here is that your mind has direct power and influence that greatly determines desirable (or undesirable) personal health.

An investment in time and dedication is required to reprogram your mind (new thinking and meditation). This is a very small investment compared to the fears, pain and high cost of traditional care. *Physician heal thyself!*

OLD AND NEW HEALTH CONCEPTS

The new holistic approach to health and treatment of disorder enlarges the framework of the old traditional way without disregarding the many benefits it has provided.

"Holistic" refers to a qualitatively different approach to health care, one that integrates mind, body and environment. It goes far beyond the allpathic practice (the treatment of the disease and its symptoms only). At the core of the holistic health movement is the desire to uproot the underlying cause that is creating the problem.

Established medical practice has become very specialized, and the emphasis is still on treating the symptoms. The holistic approach includes searching for the causes as well as treating the symptoms, with concern given to the whole patient.

Let's consider the ways health care is perceived by the traditional and New Age holistic health practitioner. While my bias is toward the holistic approach, I will try to objectively state the basic assumptions of both to give you, the reader, an overview.

TRADITIONAL HEALTH CARE	HOLISTIC HEALTH CARE
Professionalism is of primary importance	Unification of body, mind and environment is first in importance.
Treatment of the symptom is very specialized.	Search for cause while treating symptoms.
Professional is usually emotionally uninvolved.	Professional's caring and sharing with client is seen as a major aid to healing.
Body seen as a machine that is in good or bad shape.	Body condition seen as totally or partially the result of a person's thoughts.
Disease or disorder seen as a real thing, an entity.	Disease or disorder seen only as a process.
Professional is decision-maker and patient is dependent.	Professional is therapeutic assistant and patient (client) is autonomous.
Body and mind are separate.	Body/mind are integrated parts of the whole.
Mind is of secondary importance in organic illness.	Mind is the equal or greater factor in all forms of disorder.
Prevention of disease is considered basically environmental (rest, exercise, drugs, immunization, etc.).	Prevention is integrated with wholeness: body, mind and spirit, with great emphasis on thoughts.
Successful treatment seen as the result of patient's body resistant functions and the skills of the professional.	Success demonstrated by the removal of the symptoms and the cause behind the symptoms. A return to full harmony.

201

The traditional medical profession has a long and distinguished record in combating physical and emotional disorders. Many substantial victories have been won, and it would be very naive and grossly unfair not to recognize these accomplishments. When a person needs treatment to correct a disorder, it is vital that a knowledgable professional address the problem. The major drawback with putting all of the emphasis on the problem is that even if corrected, it or other related problems may physicalize unless the patient is helped at the first level of resistance: cause.

Holistic health care offers solutions to the manifested problem while searching for the underlying cause. While this writer is excited about the unlimited potential of the New Age Holistic Health approach, I am aware there are some potential problems associated with the movement. Like anything in the process of transformation, a few charlatans have entered the field. Also, some very sincere but possibly misguided individuals have instituted very unusual methods of disease prevention or cure that may not prove to be sound and beneficial in the final analysis.

Just as traditional medical professionals are either competent, incompetent or somewhere in between, so it is with the New Age practitioner. Before submitting to any kind of treatment, preventive measures, diet plans, etc., a person should interview the practitioner to gain insights into the nature of the man or woman as well as learn more about their professional methods. It also may be a very good idea to ask for the names of recent clients whom you can contact concerning their results from treatment. You must have trust in the professional who is assisting you, while at the same time fully trusting yourself to discern what is good for you and what isn't. When you learn to trust your intuition, you will be able to knowingly choose what is right for you.

SPIRITUAL MIND HEALING

Miraculous healings have been reported and documented by members of many religions. The incidents have become so numerous that it is difficult for anyone, except the dyed-in-the-wool atheist to refute the growing evidence of spiritual healings.

Science is often disturbed by the unexplainable. A scientist can only use knowledge that is systematic and organized and constant. Spiritual healings are occurrences that are extremely difficult to define and measure. However, the metaphysician is thrilled that slowly but surely science is leading everyone to the one great metaphysical deduction: the physical universe is One. Mind is One. The fact that all of us can communicate, even when there is a language barrier, establishes the Unity of all Minds. Mind is individualized but is never individual. There is only One Universal Mind and it is individualized billions of times in all life. This is often a difficult transcendental idea to understand. Sometimes to grasp this concept it helps if we contemplate the ocean. Let's look at the Pacific Ocean. There is only one Pacific Ocean and yet there are countless zillions of drops of water within the mighty Pacific Ocean. One major force supports untold water and life. Each single drop of sea water is an individualized part of the whole.

Metaphysically speaking, each of us is an individual part of that One Life which is Universal. In being a part of that which unites everything, we are part of each other and in-

203

dividualized parts of the Whole. Jesus' words, "I am the vine and ye are the branches," illustrates this point perfectly.

Why does spiritual healing appear erratic? Why aren't the results of Spiritual Mind Healing uniform? At first, these questions may confuse the truth student. Does God favor one and not another? The ultimate answer must be that the Universe plays no favorites; the results are in the demonstration. What may appear to be erratic or random healings are actually the result of perfect scientific treatments. If God does bless Jim with a healing while withholding perfect health from Janet (and students of the Mind accept no selective concept of Creative Intelligence,) then favorable results, or the lack of same, must be in the healing treatment itself.

Three persons experiencing disease or disorder may take three different mental positions with regard to Spiritual/ Mind healing. Person One may believe that this concept of healing is absurd. All trust is put in conventional health care, and no spiritual work is acted upon. Such a person negates the power, and unless a true believer intercedes and does effective treatment on this person's behalf, spiritual healing is unlikely. Spirit only turns to us as we turn to It. It has unrestricted power, but it takes individualized belief to put this power into action on a personal basis.

Person Two may have a greater understanding of spiritual treatment and may seek spiritual treatment. However, if the level of belief in healing is not stronger than the preoccupation with the disorder, spiritual healing may not be demonstrated. As Napoleon Hill has pointed out, *"What the mind of man can conceive and believe, it can achieve."* You can achieve whatever results you seek, but first you must conceive the reality you desire and truly believe (this means true feeling behind the words). Only then will it be your reality.

Now, let us look at person Three and marvel at a Spiritual Mind Healing demonstrated out of faith. This person's words were acted upon, not because he is intrinsically better than his fellows—no, not at all. The reason behind the success came from the perfect treatment. *The answer is within the prayer itself!*

In considering these three hypothetical persons and their individual beliefs and approaches to spiritual healing, it becomes more evident what is behind the "blessing" of perfect harmony. One person has no time for "spiritual stuff"; another sees the merit in such treatment but is not able to demonstrate full belief; while still another turns "spiritual stuff" into a miraculous blessing through perfect Spiritual/ Mind action.

THE CHOICE IS YOURS:
THINK YOURSELF HEALTHY
OR WORRY YOURSELF SICK

To learn to stop worrying is to reap the reward that is health and happiness. All worry is the result of the chief culprit of Total Success: Fear. Worry never helped you in any positive way or corrected any of life's situations. It is one of the most futile activities a person can engage in; yet, countless millions of people unproductively spend billions of hours in this unholy pursuit every day of their lives.

We have already discussed the life-enrichening results a broad imagination can bring. As with all great mind tools, imagination can also be perverted and misused. Worry is the practice of negative imagination. Positive thinking is the route to emotional and physical freedom. Negative thinking (and worry is negative thinking personified) is the steep, downhill path that winds down to emotional instability and imbalance, which in turn can manifest in some physical disorder.

The only positive action concerning worry is to stop the dreadful practice—immediately! But how can this be done, you ask? By fixing your thoughts on the positive! Your mind cannot think about two opposites at the exact same time. We can think about thousands of things in the course of a single day, but always one at a time. By seeing worry for the mental and emotional troublemaker that it really is and realizing nothing good results from this negative practice, we can replace worry with the right mental equivalent. Choose the positive thought that will replace the worry. Worry comes out of fear. Associated with fear are the destructive duo (destructive and dangerous to us only when we allow them to have influence in our life) lack and limitation.

When we feel trapped (by an unloving relationship, a dead-end job, etc.), we feel limited—our freedom appears to be restricted. When we feel lack (not enough money, the absence of perfect health, not enough love, etc.), we feel deprived—our good appears to be withheld. Limitation and lack create more fear, which in turn occupies the mind with worry.

Here are just a few common worries and the right mental equivalents (affirmations) that you can use to stop the worry process.

Worry: "I don't have enough money."
Positive Affirmation: **"I give thanks for the money I now have and the ever-increasing abundance that is coming to me. I take the right steps to keep the flow coming."**

Worry: "I'm not appreciated or loved."
Positive Affirmation: **"I'm always appreciated and I am always loved because I am loving. My life is filled with love and joy."**

Worry: "My physical (mental) health is deteriorating."
Positive Affirmation: **"Disease or disorders of any type are the result of unease and imbalance in my mind. I now commit myself to the positive thoughts and actions that rid my mind of all such imbalance. Perfect health is mine."**

Of course, I realize that worry is not confined to one simple sentence. The mind, when permitted to dwell on the negative, can conjure up all kinds of worry-laden thoughts. Fear of losing one's health could lead to worry about becoming a burden to others. An elderly person may begin to see herself (himself) in a nursing home, bedridden, helpless, etc. The point here is the single sentence about lack of mental/physical health is the negative core belief that then releases many other negative and stressful images. To reprogram the mind with the right mental equivalent can convert the wrong (worrysome) thought. We can and should reduce it to the core thought (usually summed up in just a few words) that puts the unproductive worry process into motion.

The key to success in the "mental battle" against worry is to reprogram a positive affirmation into your subconscious the very second your words and/or thoughts reflect a worrysome attitude.

207

Out with the negative and in with the positive! *You won't miss if you'll work with this!!*

THE BODY AS A PROCESS

When one looks upon the body as one unit that is constantly in process, it is easier to understand the patterns of health or disorder.

The body reacts (feels) the mind's joy, love, self-esteem, happiness, grief, self-pity, anger, etc. Joy and hate and all the emotions in between begin in mind and then are "experienced" in the body. The body is a majestic marvel of nature, and yet it is always subservient to our thoughts.

Many world health professionals are beginning to view the body as a process. In her important book on personal and social transformation, *The Aquarian Conspiracy*,* Marilyn Ferguson paints this dynamic body process picture with her words: *"Western medicine is beginning to recognize that the body is a process—a bioelectric whirlpool, sensitive to positive ions, cosmic rays, trace minerals in our diet, free electricity from power generators. Picturing the body at its dynamic level helps us to make sense of otherwise puzzling controversies."*

When viewing the body as a process, it is easy to see disease as a process. Healing, too, can then be seen as a process. We often say, "Jimmy came down with the flu" or "he caught a cold." In viewing these two common disorders as a process, we could copy Dr. Ellerbroek's description of disease as a process and say, "Jimmy is in the process of experiencing the cold or flu experience."

*The Aquarian Conspiracy © 1980 by Marilyn Ferguson, J.P. Tarcher, Inc. Los Angeles, CA

Wallace Ellerbroek is a psychiatrist and a former surgeon who has had much success in treating several diseases by teaching his patients to both confront and accept the process. He believes one can acknowledge the disorder, accept it as presently evident and then work to dissolve it by removing the patient's energy from it. When this is done, often the disorder completely disappears. Dr. Ellerbroek explains his concept of disease: "We doctors seem to have a predilection for nouns in naming diseases (epilepsy, measles, brain tumor), and because these things *deserve* nouns as names, then obviously they are real things to us. If you take one of these nouns—measles—and make it into a verb, then it becomes, 'Mrs. Jones, your little boy appears to be measling,' which opens both your mind and hers to the concept of a disease as a process."

When we reexamine our concept toward health and disease, it becomes apparent health and disease don't just happen to us—they are not "something out there that we catch!" They are processes that are activated by mental/physical balance or imbalance, harmony or disharmony, always directly influenced by our present state of consciousness. Wrong (negative) thinking can manifest itself into a process of imbalance and disorder. Positive (pro-life) thinking manifests itself as positive living and harmony, which in turn induces the process of optimum health. The bottom line, as always, is that everything (whether we judge it positively, negatively or indifferently) begins in Mind.

BETTER HEALTH STARTS WITH AN IDEA

While most people, health professionals and lay persons alike, concede that thoughts have influence on how they physically feel, many cannot comprehend how it is that thought can actually affect their total environment. Almost all people can grasp the concept that the body is an interconnected unit. Our environment is not so easily perceived as an integral part of us.

The environment on Earth is animal, mineral and vegetable, combined with water. That is it! This is the basic stuff from which all other things (buildings, homes, cars, guns, food, jewelry, clothes, highways, candy, toothpaste, etc.) are made of, all created and molded by the hand of man, using Universal Wisdom to shape his environment.

On the individual level, we also create and shape our personal environment. To grow and harvest wheat, corn and soy beans, the farmer plants wheat, corn or soybean seeds. If he plants corn seed, he gets corn (provided that he properly plants, tills and waters the soil). He does not plant corn and get tomatoes. As he sows, he also reaps.

We are surrounded by an environment that we may think is good or bad, beautiful or ugly. We may also judge it friendly or hostile, but in the final analysis it is to us as we are to it. The person in the process of experiencing "sickness" may rebel against this fact. He may say, "I did not choose to have this disease. My illness was work-related (or in some other way contracted)." While it is highly unlikely that anyone, except someone expressing acute self-hatred, would knowingly plant seeds of mental or physical disorder, they are a byproduct or some spiritual/mental lack or imbalance. Just what kind of resentment, envy, worry or other negative thoughts/feelings are harbored deep beneath the surface may not be readily evident. One thing is certain, if you believe that health and disease are processes that are first created in your mind, you may be certain that all forms of disorder are the effect of some kind of imbalance, whether it is readily recognizable or not.

If we can choose love, happiness, full self-expression, abundance and health, is it not then logical to state that we do indeed have the power to create our very environment? I think it is!

All life's experiences confirm ideas and thoughts from within and not from without. If you like what you're witnessing in your personal environment, you are living by the Principles that govern the Universe. If you don't like all that you see, don't despair. You have within you the power to change it! This is the secret of the ages!

PRAYER AND MEDITATION FOR BETTER HEALTH

Prayer changes things, and the most important thing it changes is the person who prays. For the believer (and some degree of belief or at least willingness is required), prayer is a powerful tool to use to maintain or restore good health. Increasing numbers of doctors are becoming aware of prayer power, and benefits available from the meditative state. Prayer is an instinctive, contemplative activity which has been practiced by truthseekers throughout the ages. Verbal or nonverbal prayer can be defined as consciously talking to God (Spirit). Meditation (another form of prayer) can be defined as listening to God.

There are five basic types of prayer. They are: supplication, contemplation, adoration, Scientific Mind Prayer and meditation.

Supplication Prayer

The prayer of supplication is practiced by "asking", "begging" or "pleading" with God. A prayer of supplication may go like this: "Dear God, my son Jimmy needs healing from his injuries in an automobile accident. Please help him and heal him."

Such prayer seeks a "yes" or "no" answer to some problem. The belief is that God can and will choose to either extend or withhold a blessing, healing, etc., depending on how "convincing" the person praying can be. It is probably the method most people, throughout time, have used when praying. It is not practiced by students of Metaphysics.

Contemplation

Contemplative prayer is a deep absorption in spiritual ideals that allows a person to feel his or her "oneness" with God and to be "inspired and lifted" in the process. Anyone who contemplates the beauty of nature feels this beautiful contemplative state of consciousness. Contemplative prayer can assist anyone in becoming more sensitive and loving.

Adoration

The conscious act of adoring God, truth, love, joy, beauty, goodness or any form of life is a powerful method to raise human consciousness and make contact with Universal Creative Intelligence. Adoration and a joyous, thanksgiving heart are a life-enhancing experience that induces much happiness into the experience of the one who is upholding and praising God, good, life. The person who loves his life and who gives thanks constantly for the joy of living, receives more good things to be thankful for.

Scientific Mind Prayer

Scientific Mind Prayer, which is also often called Scientific Mind Treatment or Spiritual Mind Treatment, is total belief in cause and effect. It is belief that there are Universal Mental Laws that will always respond to us, as we "believe". Scientific prayer does not try to change God's mind about any given situation, but rather to invoke change in the mind of the person praying or the one being prayed for. A scientific approach to prayer is rooted in the belief that the Universe never plays favorites and will respond to anyone and everyone to the exact degree that a person's belief will allow. Scientific prayer can be summed up in just one biblical verse: "It is done unto thee as thee believes."

Meditation

Meditation is often regarded as a process that is somehow not the same as prayer. We often say *prayer and meditation*. In reality, meditation is just another form of praying. It is a continued and constant alignment of thought. Meditation can transform a person's awareness from the levels of emotion, rational mind and body, to contemplation upon and receptiveness to spiritual ideas. It is Contemplative Prayer (already defined) carried several levels deeper. It is, perhaps, the best method human beings can practice to renew and rejuvenate the body, mind and emotions. Deep meditation can also be the "space" to receive answers to all of life's challenges and situations. Life-enrichening results are obtainable to those who meditate daily.

MEDITATION TECHNIQUES

THE TIME, PLACE, AND LENGTH: Try to arrange the same time and place to meditate. While some meditate for one or more hours daily, noticeable results are available to those who meditate for much shorter periods. A minimum of fifteen minutes daily is recommended by most meditators.

THE POSITION: While there are many meditative positions (the full lotus, the partial lotus, etc.), a person must feel comfortable and be fully relaxed. Most Americans and others in western civilization do not feel comfortable in the various "pretzel positions" achieved by their eastern brethren. Sitting with the back very straight in a high-back chair is a popular "western position." Sit well back in the chair with your feet flat on the floor. Keep the spine straight and balanced, the shoulders hanging relaxed from the spine and the hands hanging relaxed from the shoulders or lying open and receptive, palms up, on the lap. This position frees the medulla oblongata (the energy center at the base of the skull) and also allows deep breathing.

MEDITATIVE CONTROLS: Decide before going into meditation what controls you desire. Are you willing to come out of meditation to answer the telephone? If not, take it off the hook. If you decide you are willing to be interrupted by a telephone, someone at the door, etc., affirm ahead of time that you will easily and effortlessly come out of the meditative state for such interruptions, take care of the matter and return to meditation. The time, place and length of your meditation should be conducive to peace and silence. However, if you must contend with passing traffic or a radio or television on in another room, just notice that there is noise in the background, let it be and go within. Soon, such noise will appear to fade away. Loud, abrasive noise may present too much resistance and should be avoided. Before going into meditation, set up your controls for coming out of meditation. Affirm that after fifteen minutes, twenty minutes, a half hour or however long your meditation time will be you will return from the subjective state of mind to the objective. It is a good idea to tell yourself that you will return fresh, alert and in full objective control to the objective state after counting to three with three deep breaths after each slow count. If you should ever return to the objective state not feeling alert and relaxed, briefly return to the meditative state and then bring yourself out again, slowly and firmly.

THE MEDITATIVE PROCESS ITSELF: There are many forms of meditation. A person can meditate on something (a desired object, happening, on God, beauty, etc.) or on nothing, entering the meditative state like an empty vessel that awaits to be filled. Before entering meditation, set your purpose. Speak your word. What do you wish to accomplish? Do you just desire energy and renewal from the process? If new energy and renewal is your goal, let your mind drift from impression to impression or at least until something interesting and revealing comes to you. Do not try to turn your mind into a blank, or complete void. Only a very few mystics seem to be able to completely empty all thoughts from their minds. A great affirmation to use if your purpose for meditating is to receive new knowledge and/or energy is: "I let go and let God, knowing the right answers and directions are coming to me."

If you wish to focus your attention on a specific event, challenge, etc., close your eyes (eyes closed is highly recommended for all types of meditation) and turn your inner vision on the object of your meditation. Without judging anything or anyone, notice what you "see" and become aware of. Whatever comes up, acknowledge it, don't put a label on it, and continue to view it from all sides that are presented. You may be amazed at the instant revelation that you receive. Even if revelation is not instantaneous, know that the right answer will become evident to you, even if days, weeks or months later. The answers will come!

If you find it difficult to enter into the meditative state, use these five meditative steps:

1. FEEL SECURE WITH YOUR MEDITATIVE EN-VIRONMENT.

2. COMPLETELY RELAX YOUR PHYSICAL BODY. (Start from the feet and slowly work up to the head, focusing your mind's eye, slowly and soothingly, on each part of the body—feet, ankles, thighs, pelvic region, etc.)

3. CALM YOUR CONSCIOUS MIND. (Don't try to intellectualize anything in the meditative process.)

4. RELAX THE MIND. (Notice that it is always active and still can be relaxed by your flowing, gentle thoughts.)

5. BE STILL. (Don't try to rid your mind of any thoughts or images. Just don't evaluate or judge anything that comes up.)

Several deep breaths can help induce the meditative state. Breathe very deeply and then exhale. With each exhale, tell yourself if you are releasing any negative concepts or "unpure thoughts" that may have entered your consciousness. With each deep breath, "see" yourself inhaling positive, pure, energized thoughts of love, happiness, health, riches and full harmony.

HEALTH RESTORATION MEDITATION

Now that I have given you some basic meditation techniques, and since this chapter is concerned with health, let me present here a healing, anti-disease meditation exercise.

Sitting in a straight-back chair with both feet flat on the floor (short people can use a telephone book to rest their feet on if required), turn one hand palm up in your lap and allow the other (if you're right-handed, let the right arm hang loose) to dangle. After going through your pre-meditation controls, put yourself into the meditation process. Go as deep into meditation as you possibly can.

Bring your full attention to the arm hanging by your side. Simply notice it. Now, feel your blood flowing down your arm. Feel it send "tingling sensations" through your arm. That's fine. Just keep being aware of the arm itself. There is no need to be concerned when your mind starts to drift away from being fixed on your hanging arm, just gently bring your attention (not your gaze—your eyes are closed) back to the hanging arm.

After keeping your attention on the hanging arm for what you believe to be one full minute (approximately one whole minute in which your mind has not wandered on to other topics and then had to be brought back—it may take you several minutes to accomplish this. That's okay, do it!), it's time to put your attention for approximately 10 to 15 seconds on each of your five fingers. Both feel your attention and "see" (with your mind's eye) your little finger. Experience it. Then, move on to the next finger, repeating the same exercise. After completing the exercise on all five fingers, experiencing your thumb lastly, place your attention on the palm of your hanging hand. For at least 30 seconds experience it. Feel it and "see it." If you notice that your mind wanders, simply bring it back to your palm. Your palm is tingling now. Good. Experience the tingle. Keep doing this. Stay aware of the palm of your hand. See it. Feel it tingle. Experience it.

Now, turn your attention, your mind's eye, to that part of your body that has given you problems (the neck, back, lungs, heart, legs, feet, head or wherever there appears to be disorder). If it is sore or aching now, zero in on the pain. Feel the pain. Let your mind's eye go inside the area of discomfort where the fire is. What color is the pain? Is it red? Reddish yellow? Burning orange? Now picture, in your mind's eye, yourself pouring a bucket of cool, clear water over the colored pain flames. See yourself putting out the fire with the cool, healing water. Feel the soothing water still the fire. "See" the flames disappear.

If pain is not being experienced and nevertheless healing is required, use the same exercise, up to the point where you put out the fire with a bucket of water. Instead, experience the problem that exists, see it, experience it and then see yourself energized by your mind. See yourself surrounded by a brilliant blue and yellow aura, a powerful blue and yellow healing light. You are surrounded by this miraculous healing light. Anything it touches, anything it comes in contact with will be healed. Keep your attention on the vision of yourself surrounded by this beautiful blue/yellow light. If your mind drifts, return it to this image. Now, see the light completely engulf the vision of you in the area of your body that needs healing. The vision of you has now disappeared, but the light is now more brilliant than ever as it makes contact with and consumes the body part that once appeared to be afflicted. See it as completely restored! Totally healed! **BELIEVE!!!**

There are many roads to good health (nutrition, sleep, exercise, preventive medicine, etc.), and the best one of all is Mind.

To learn how to think healthy is to learn how to love and live healthfully in blessed harmony and ease.

*"Love everyone unconditionally,
including yourself . . . "*

—KEN KEYES, JR.

Chapter Ten

LOVE IS THE ONLY POWER

Every person is born with the need to be loved unconditionally. None of us ever outgrows this need. The more love we experience, the greater our opportunity to self-actualize. Love is the greatest power—nay, the only *real* power—and love is the answer to every challenge that human beings face.

Love is by far the most important source of personal happiness. Love is overwhelmingly more significant than money, fame, status or any other form of satisfaction that we may desire.

If love is vital to our experiencing joy and happiness, as it definitely is, why do so many men and women have so much difficulty giving and receiving this blessed gift? The answer is we are not experiencing enough love because we don't know how to love. Too often we become addicted to wants, desires, and emotional responses that are diametrically in opposition to love, joy and self-fulfillment. Why do we so often alienate ourselves from the very things we need to live life fully (love, peace, happiness)? Ken Keyes, Jr., in his inspired, conscious-raising book, *Handbook to Higher Consciousness,* provides great insight into this question.

Following are Ken's words on Secrets of Happiness and the Laws of Higher Consciousness, including his insights into Unconditional Love, from the *Handbook.*

Why do we have lives filled with turmoil, desperation, and anxiety? Why are we always pushing ourselves and

221

others? Why do we have only small dribbles of peace, love, and happiness? Why is it that human beings are characterized by bickering and turmoil that make animals' relationships with their own species seem peaceful in comparison? The answer is so simple—but it is sometimes difficult for us to really understand because *almost every way we were taught to work toward happiness only reinforces the feelings and activities that make us unhappy.*

This is a central point that must be understood. The ways we were taught to be happy can't possibly work. Unless we see this point clearly, we cannot progress to higher consciousness. Here's why.

Most of us assume that our desires (backed up by our emotional feelings) are the true guides to doing the things that will make us happy. **But no one has yet found happiness by using emotion-backed desires as guides.** Flashes of pleasure, yes; happiness, no.

Our wants and desires are so seductive . . . . They masquerade as "needs" that must be satisfied so we can be happy at last. They lead us from one illusion of happiness to another. Some of us tell ourselves, "If I can just get to be president of this corporation, I will be happy." But have you ever seen a really happy president? His outside drama may feature beautiful yachts, Cadillacs, Playboy bunnies—but is he really happy inside? Has his ulcer gone away?

We constantly tell ourselves such things as, "If I could just go back to school and acquire more knowledge—perhaps get a Master's degree—then I will be happy." But are people with Master's degrees or Ph.D.'s any happier than the rest of us? It is beautiful to acquire knowledge but it is misleading to expect it to bring us peace, love, and happiness. We tell ourselves, "If I could only find the right person to love, then I would be happy." So we search for someone who our addictions tell us is the right person—and we experience some pleasurable moments. *But since we don't know how to love,* the relationships gradually deteriorates. Then we decide we didn't have the right person after all! As we grow into higher consciousness, we discover that it is more important to *be the right person* than to find the right person.

We must deeply understand why *all* of our negative emotions are misleading guides to effective action in life situations. *Our negative emotions are simply the result of an extensive pattern of scars and wounds that we have experienced.* And these emotional wounds lead us to perceive *differences* that make us uptight instead of *similarities* that enable us to understand and love. The present programming of our emotions makes us perceive other people (and the conditions of the world around us) as threats—potentially dangerous to our well-being. We then respond with adrenalin, faster heart beat, increased blood sugar, and other jungle survival responses that prepare us for fight or flight. We are trapped in our ways of perceiving the world around us.

But no one (or no situation) need be felt as an emotional threat or danger when we see things with the clearer perception of higher consciousness. Think of the most threatening situation you have felt in the last day or two. Are you about to lose your job? Is the person for whom you feel the most love paying more attention to someone else than to you? Do you have unpaid bills that you cannot take care of? Do you have a pain that could be cancer? Now, these problems either have

223

solutions—or they don't. Either you can do something about them here and now—or you can't. If you can do something here and now about them, then do it—even if it's just a first step. It saps your energy to be worried or anxious about a problem. Do what you can do—but don't be addicted to the results or you will create more worry for yourself. If you can't do anything about a problem here and now, then why make yourself uncomfortable and drain your energy by worrying about it? *It is part of the here and nowness of your life.* That's *what is*—here and now. Worry, anxiety, or other unpleasant emotions are absolutely unnecessary—and simply lower your insight and the effectiveness of your actions.

You must absolutely convince yourself of the lack of utility of these draining emotions. You must see your unnecessary worrying as depriving you of the flowing effectiveness and joyousness that you should have in your life. As long as you think that these negative emotions have any function whatsoever, you will retard your growth into higher consciousness. If you do not hassle yourself emotionally *when the outside world does not conform with your inside programming* (your desires, expectations, demands, or models of how the world should treat you) you will have so much energy that you probably will sleep fifty percent less. You will be joyous and loving, and really appreciate each moment of your life—no matter what's happening in the world of people and situations outside you.

Where and how did we get this emotional programming? Almost all of it was acquired in the first few years of life. For example, when we were very young, we had the experience of mother forcefully taking a perfume bottle from our tiny fingers and at the same time sending out bad vibrations based on her desire not to have her perfume bottle broken. We cried. Through being painfully pushed around, dominated, told what to do, and controlled when we were babies, we developed our emotionally intense security, sensation, and power programs. Many of our emotion-backed programs came from repeated moral directives or statements about how things "should" be. We developed a "self" consciousness with robot-like emotional responses to protect the "survival" of this separate self.

So we become emotionally programmed to feel that we must have power to control and manipulate people in order to be happy. We eventually become very finely attuned to the actions or vibrations of any person or situation that even remotely threatens our power addictions—our ability to manipulate and control people and things around us.

As we reach physical maturity and our biocomputer (or brain) is able to function more perceptively, *we have all the power we need.* But our biocomputer (backed up by the full repertory of our emotions) is still *programmed to compensate for the power deficiency* we experienced when we were infants and young children. We now need to learn to flow with the people and things around us. But our power addiction keeps us from loving people because we perceive them as objects that may threaten our power, prestige, or pecking order. If we want to love and be loved, we can't be addicted to power—or to anything else.

As conscious beings the only thing we need to find happiness in life is to perceive clearly *who we are* (we are pure consciousness and not the social roles we are acting out), and exactly what are *the real conditions,* here and now, of our lives. How basically simple is our problem! But to achieve this clear perception of ourselves and the world around us takes constant inner work. And this means developing the habit of *emotionally* accepting whatever is here and now in our lives. For only an emotionally calm biocomputer can see clearly and wisely, and come up with effective ways to interact with people and situations.

Our power addiction is only one example of the happiness-destroying programming that we put into our biocomputers when we were too young to perceive the realities of the world in which we lived. Although we now have the basic capacity for clear perception, the operating instructions we gave our biocomputer anchor us to the lower levels. And so we're unconsciously trapped.

Here and now is the reality in our lives—and it is only from the conditions of the present that our future can be generated. But our present addictions, demands, and expectations (the programming of our biocomputer) dominate our consciousness and force us to spend most of the time we are awake (and most of the time we are dreaming) in protesting and pouting about the here and now situation in our lives. This lowers our perceptiveness and keeps us from finding effective solutions to our problems. The Living Love Way to Higher Consciousness shows us how to break through this trap, to free ourselves, and to find our full potential as human beings.

Your growth into higher consciousness should begin by fully understanding the importance of becoming one with the Law of Higher Consciousness:

**Love everyone unconditionally—
including yourself.**

This law can enable you to find the hidden splendor within yourself and others. Unfortunately, we have never been taught how to love unconditionally. Almost all of our loving has been motivated by emotional desires programmed into us at an early age. Most of our love experiences have taught us we must earn or deserve love before we can have it—and that others must deserve our love. This is conditional love—it is like a barter or a business transaction. It is no wonder that our well-meaning but unskilled attempts to love usually end up in separation and alienation. We have been taught to place conditions on our love: "If you really loved me you would . . . "—and then we use one of our addictions to finish the sentence. This is an exchange—it is not unconditional love.

What is unconditional love? It is not, "I can love you if you do what my emotional programming—my addictions—says I want you to do." It is just love. Just, "I love you because you are there. I love you because you are part of the nowness of my life. I love you because although our bodies and minds may be on different trips, on the consciousness level all of us are alike in our humanness. We are one."

Real love is simply accepting another person. Completely and unconditionally! We experience things from his or her psychic space. It is like seeing the world through his or her eyes. Whatever he or she is going through—whatever he or she is feeling—we have been there, too—at some time in our lives.

When we love, we view others as unfolding beings in their journey toward higher consciousness. We realize that no matter how intensely we strive for worldly attainments, we all seek love and oneness on the consciousness

227

level. We are all on the journey to higher consciousness. Some of us are hearing the messages life offers us and are working *consciously* to eliminate our addictions. Others are not progressing rapidly because they do not yet know how to consciously work on themselves.

We must also learn to *love ourselves*—right here and now. We need to feel that no matter how horrible we have judged our past actions, *each day our life begins anew*. We have at all times been lovable. A child may be naughty, but he is always lovable. And so we are all children as long as we are programmed with our lower consciousness addictions. So we must accept the melodramas we get involved in as we live out our current crop of addictions. This, too, is a part of life and growth.

Every part of the system of Living Love is designed to help you learn to love everyone unconditionally— including yourself. You only need to plant the Living Love seeds in your consciousness and they will automatically sprout. Do not berate yourself because you are not enlightened by the third Tuesday of next month. The more you learn to love and accept yourself, the more you will realize that you are doing exactly what you need to do to provide yourself with experiences to grow into higher consciousness.

How can you love others if you do not love yourself? The love you have for yourself and the love you have for "another" are building blocks joining together within you to create the beautiful edifice of real love.

Learning to love unconditionally means getting free of interference from our programmed addictions—those emotion-backed demanding instructions to our bio-computer. This enables us to perceive clearly what is here and now—to evaluate wisely—and to act effectively to do whatever we want to do about it. The key to this is the instant emotional acceptance of the here and now—*the emotional acceptance of the previously unacceptable.*

When our emotions are triggered, we cannot perceive clearly our actual life situation. Our biocomputer then sends a flow of information to our consciousness in which separation and alienation are emphasized. We create a horribly warped evaluation of the here and now based on our addictive programming. When this happens, we magnify differences and suppress similarities between ourselves and "others." And this destroys our ability to love unconditionally.

We all know that just having the desire to love is not enough. As far back as we can remember we have been aware of the importance of love in our lives. We know that lack of love is responsible for most of the unhappiness in the world—for difficulties in getting along with other people, for pollution, prejudice, wars, and other individual and group crimes against humanity. But what can we do about it?

The Law of Higher Consciousness suggests a practical guide for the Aquarian Age:

You add suffering to the world
just as much when you take offense
as when you give offense.

Ken also offers these two definitions of happiness and love:

"Happiness happens when your consciousness is not dominated by addictions and demands—and you experience life as a PARADE OF PREFERENCES."

229

"The purpose of our lives is to be free of all addictive traps and thereby become one with the ocean of living love."

Reprinted with permission from Handbook to Higher Consciousness *by Ken Keyes, Jr., Fifth Edition, Copyright 1975 by Living Love Center, St. Mary, Kentucky 40063.*

LOVE STARTS WITH YOU

To experience more love in your life, you must first become more loving. Again, the biblical verse, "As ye sow, so shall ye reap," speaks the eternal truth. You can't have love unless you *are* love. You must *be* the thing that you want! That's the way it works! The principle is simple in theory and it does really work. For some of us, *Practicing the Principle* does not always seem to come that easy.

When we think other people are the source of the love we reach for, we make them into love gods. We expect our mates, children, parents and friends to love us and provide us security. Sooner or later we come to believe that they are "withholding" love from us. When this happens, we feel terribly insecure and threatened. We set ourselves up so that our whole world can be broken by the words or actions of a "loved one." There can be no happiness in such addictive behavior. To make other people the source of your love is to live your life as a complete emotional dependent, always moments away from deep depression due to the words or actions of another.

FEELINGS OF SEPARATION

When we experience separateness, we become anxious.

230

Feelings of separateness are the cause of all anxiety. To be separate is to feel cut off, to experience helplessness, to know alienation.

Erich Fromm, the renowned psychoanalyst, in his best-selling book, *The Art of Loving*, makes this dramatic statement on separateness: "The deepest need of man is the need to overcome his separateness, to leave the prison of his aloneness . . . man—of all ages and cultures—is confronted with the solution of one and the same question: The question of how to overcome separateness, how to achieve unity, how to transcend one's own individual life and find at-onement."

The world famous psychoanalyst's words strike true. Feelings of separation leave us feeling unloved and unwanted. We must be able to relate and be close to others and still should never transfer our power to them. Unhappiness will result in either being separated from others or by clinging to them and making them the source of our love and happiness. What may first appear to be two totally different approaches actually will produce the very same unfulfilling condition.

Only a "whole" person who is in love with his life is capable of unification with all other forms of life. We feel separateness first within, and this leads to feelings of outer alienation. Total unification within, in mind and spirit, creates unity with all that we come in contact with.

FREE CHOICE IS YOUR RIGHT

I am in total agreement with Ken Keyes, Jr., that unconditional love is the reality of higher consciousness, and at the same time, you have a right to choose your lover, your

*ART OF LOVING by Erich Fromm, © 1956, Harper & Row Publishers, NY, NY

friends, your individual experiences. Free will is a precious God-ordained gift that we ought to always cherish and exercise continuously.

The apple and orange are both delicious fruits. In their perfect state they are beautiful, tasty and nourishing. In choosing to eat the apple, you need not, in any way, make it better or more important than the orange. You simply were given an option and exercised your choice. While people would not find it too difficult to choose between an apple or orange, strictly from personal preferences, not making the other wrong, we usually pass harsher judgments on other experiences and people in our life. In the book of Genesis, the Bible tells the symbolic story of how God created mankind. Adam and Eve's fall from grace followed their eating from the tree of *the knowledge of good and evil.* To make something "good", one runs the risk of creating its opposite—"bad" or evil. To believe something is "right" is to consider something else is "wrong". Be careful with such definitions. To consistently judge things, happenings and other humans is to increase a sense of "duality" in your experience. Choosing one experience rather than another, or the choice to be with a certain person rather than another, can be very rewarding, without being judgmental. Preferences allow you to exercise your free-will and free-choice without making anyone or anything else wrong.

Love everyone (really "FEEL" love for everyone) on a "universal" level. Stop judging and release resentments and at the same time choose to personalize your lovingness with those you prefer to be with. This puts the freedom into free-choice!

SUCCESSFUL RELATIONSHIPS BEGIN WITH YOU

Our lives revolve around many relationships. We interact with mates, children, parents, employees, employers, friends, clients, and the check-out girl at the grocery store. Before we can have a successful relationship with anyone, we first need a perfect personal relationship. Because our self-image determines how we relate to anyone and everyone we come into contact with, we absolutely must unconditionally love ourselves first. The ultimate púrpose of any successful relationship is to give, receive and share value. This is only possible if we perceive the gift of ourselves as loving, supportive, powerful and worthy. According to Ken Keyes, Jr., every person that we meet is either our teacher or our lover. If this be true, and I sense that it is, we, too, are teachers. The most beautiful, intimate relationship is the one in which you and another have chosen to be together in a teacher/student and lover/beloved relationship.

If you addictively "need" a relationship with a certain person, you are courting trouble. A recent popular love song uses this verse to describe a love relationship—"I was half, now I'm whole." While this concept may sound romantic put to music, in reality it does not work. If you believe you're only "half" a person who is looking for your other "half", your life isn't going to work very well. Two human's halves make "two halves" and not one whole! Nobody else is the source of your loving feelings. While it is true that love desires to be shared and given away, and love always wants other people to feel its healing and inspirational touch, your "love well" is deep inside of you. It is never "out there!" You can't get love, you can only *be* love.

233

Don't rush into any kind of relationship. Work on yourself. Feel yourself, experience yourself and love yourself. Do this first and you will soon attract that special loving other. Then together, you can share the adventure that is life.

The key to loving transformation is to know that love and relationships start with you. The cause of your personal happiness is you. Giving of yourself freely and by choice can be a beautiful expression of your love. Giving up your personal power and placing your quest for fulfillment in the hands of another will not work. Self-suppression and love are totally incompatible.

HIGH CONSCIOUS RELATIONSHIPS

Ken Keyes, Jr., the author of the New Age transformation book, *Handbook to Higher Consciousness,* is also the author of several other remarkable guidebooks, one of which, *A Conscious Person's Guide to Relationship*, is a definitive guide to New Thought relationships. I am deeply thankful to be able to quote from this remarkable work. Here are, in Ken's words, the "Living Love" approach to more creative, more loving relationships.

GO INTO A RELATIONSHIP TO COOPERATE WITH EACH OTHER IN THE GREAT ADVENTURE OF LIFE

Many people don't seem to have a definite notion of what motivates them to go into a relationship. They seem to feel that the purpose of the relationship is the relationship itself. Yet most of us do have specific things in mind as we search around for a partner. See

234

if you can identify with one or more of the following:

"I'd like to have a sexual partner."

"I feel more secure money-wise when I'm married to someone."

"It's really nice to have a companion so that I'm not lonely."

"It will make my parents feel better when I'm married."

"I want to have children."

"I can use my relationship for spiritual growth."

"I'm tired of dating around; it's time to settle down."

"I want someone I can show off to my friends."

"I need someone to earn money and take care of me if I'm sick."

"It helps me feel complete."

Let me again point out that I don't want to make any of the above ideas about going into a relationship either right or wrong. But I'd like to share with you what I tell myself in this area. Living with someone gives me the opportunity to cooperate in the great adventure of life. This tunes my mind in to an awareness of who likes to be with me and to cooperate in the things I enjoy doing. It also helps me look at whether I enjoy cooperating in the things she likes to do.

Of course, I don't expect anything to be one hundred percent—life isn't like that. I thank the universe if the person I'm living with likes to cooperate with me in three-fourths of the things I like to do in creating my adventure of living on planet Earth. As Goddard so beautifully put it, "Happiness is the art of making a bouquet of those flowers within reach."

FALLING IN LOVE IS NOT A
BASIS FOR INVOLVEMENT

"Falling in love is not a basis for involvement? That's crazy," you may say to yourself. I must admit that it does sound crazy—especially coming from the founder of the Living Love Way to happiness—but perhaps it's crazy wisdom.

The problem is that ninety-nine percent of us operate from a great deficiency of love. We often didn't experience enough love in our childhood, and our heart hungers for this precious feeling. We live continuously with this longing for love. We are on the lookout for people who seem to be able to accept and love us. We are like hungry tigers that haven't eaten for a month. And when we find a person who feels some love for us, it's a tremendous event. We feel love is so scarce that we have to do something about it. Cage it. Tie it up. Don't let it get away!

. . . By working on our addictive models of how the world should be, we begin to radiate an ever-widening acceptance and love. The people around us begin to tune in to the way we are increasingly creating unconditional love for them. They like being with someone who is living love. It's like finding an oasis in the desert.

In my own experience, I found that as I learned to love unconditionally, I began to create and live in a world of love. I've now learned to operate my mind and heart so that I can stay in love with everybody—most of the time.

. . . So if you are effectively working on yourself to

love everyone unconditionally, you cannot use love as a basis for involvement. You'll be loving everybody—but you can't live with everybody you love.

. . . Although romantic love is a great feeling, building a relationship on it is like building a house on quicksand—the foundation is not stable. Unconditional love gives a stable foundation to a relationship. And it means just what it says. No conditions—no strings attached to my love. No matter what you say or do, I will continue loving you. I may not like what you do, but my love is unconditional and will not be affected—not even if our involvement changes.

CAN YOU SHARE LIFE'S GAMES IN A WAY THAT WILL CONTRIBUTE TO YOUR MUTUAL WELL-BEING?

. . . We often focus on the additional things our partner "should" or "could" offer us in the relationship. Our logical intellect may addictively insist on a "fair" or a "50-50" approach. This just causes arguments in which we make ourselves "right"—but we lose intimacy and happiness.

Your ego may create the illusion that if you constantly point out the deficiencies of your partner, s/he will be motivated to give you more. You may have noticed that this isn't effective. You may try to bribe, or coerce him or her into giving you more than s/he is giving at the moment. This really won't work well, either. But if you're doing these things in your relationship, don't put yourself down. These "right-wrong" games of the ego-mind are only a stage of growth. Be gentle and compassionate with yourself.

To emotionally demand things of your partner is human; to let go of separating demands is divine. As you tune more deeply in to your spiritual wisdom which has often been lying unused in your heart, you will begin to realize that your partner can only be where s/he is at each moment. And if real change (instead of coerced, surface, phony change) is to take place, it is only through love that s/he will create more perceptiveness of your needs and desires, and more willingness to do what you want.

The best way to help your partner experience greater love is **for you to create in yourself an experience of greater love for him or her**—and I mean do it first. And I mean do it continuously. And I mean to keep doing it whether or not you get the "results" you are looking for. To really get "results", you must strip your love of all its conditionality.

DON'T EXPECT THE RELATIONSHIP
TO MAKE YOU HAPPY

The opportunity to live with another human being is one of life's greatest gifts. You damage and bruise this gift by your demands and expectations that the relationship make you happy. Sorry, but no one's going to rescue you. The number and strength of your addictions is far more important in creating your personal experience of happiness or unhappiness than who you're with!

. . . Emotionally accepting does not mean that you don't try to change something. It just means that you

238

don't waste your energy in anger, irritation, resentment, fear and frustration. You intelligently focus your energy into making whatever changes are possible without setting up new problems in your life.

"I LOVE YOU" REALLY MEANS "WHEN I'M WITH YOU, I'M IN TOUCH WITH THE BEAUTIFUL, CAPABLE AND LOVABLE PARTS OF ME."

. . . What is really happening inside my nervous system when I say, "I love you?" What's happening is that when I am with you, things you say and do **help me experience parts of me that I regard as beautiful, capable and lovable.** In other words, **what I am loving is my own experience of me.** You're mirroring me and are letting me see the beautiful, capable and lovable parts of me.

INVOLVEMENT, YES; ADDICTION, NO.

To get the most from your relationship, you'll find it helpful to distinguish between **involvement** with a person and **addiction** to being with the person. Let's define these two key terms. Involvement means "I share my life with you." Addiction means "I create the experience that I am lost without you. I need you to be happy."

Involvement means spending a lot of time together. Addiction means creating emotion-backed demands in my head that dictate what my partner should say and do—it means "ownership". Involvement means that I

239

choose to share a large part of my life with my beloved and build a mutual reality together.

INVOLVEMENT	ADDICTION	WHAT'S HAPPENING
Maximum	Maximum	Romantic or Possessive Love
Minimum	Maximum	Broken Heart
Minimum	Minimum	Friends
Maximum	Minimum	All The Goodies. No Unhappiness.

ASK FOR WHAT YOU WANT, BUT DON'T BE ADDICTED TO GETTING IT

> *Ask for what you want,*
> *Enjoy what you get,*
> *Work on any difference.*

. . . Often we ask for what we want in a way that implies blame or right-wrong if our partner does not give us what we ask for. Or we may feel, "I've been real courageous and up-front by asking for what I want, and you'd better reward me." We can see this as manipulative and unskillful, for it is a product of the separate self that reflects a "me-vs.-you" consciousness.

DEVELOP YOUR AWARENESS OF THE CONSTANT BEAUTY AND PERFECTION OF YOURSELF AND YOUR PARTNER

. . . when you deeply love other people, you clearly experience how okay they are as human beings. Your own addictions may not let you see that the same thing applies to you. But you, too, are beautiful the way you are, with all of your foibles, failings and flatulence. And who knows—if you can successfully help your partner accept himself or herself when being genuine, perhaps your partner will someday be able to help you to accept yourself as beautiful, capable and lovable when you are being genuine.

THE TWELVE PATHWAYS
To Unconditional Love and Happiness

FREEING MYSELF

1. I am freeing myself from security, sensation, and power addictions that make me try to forcefully control situations in my life, and thus destroy my serenity and keep me from loving myself and others.

2. I am discovering how my consciousness-dominating addictions create my illusory version of the changing world of people and situations around me.

3. I welcome the opportunity (even if painful) that my minute-to-minute experience offers me to become aware of the addictions I must reprogram to be liberated from my robot-like emotional patterns.

BEING HERE NOW

4. I always remember that I have everything I need to enjoy my here and now—unless I am letting my consciousness be dominated by demands and expectations based on the dead past or the imagined future.

5. I take full responsibility here and now for everything I experience, for it is my own programming that creates my actions and also influences the reactions of people around me.

6. I accept myself completely here and now and consciously experience everything I feel, think, say, and do (including my emotion-backed addictions) as a necessary part of my growth into higher consciousness.

INTERACTING WITH OTHERS

7. I open myself genuinely to all people by being willing to fully communicate my deepest feelings, since hiding in any degree keeps me stuck in my illusion of separateness from other people.

8. I feel with loving compassion the problems of others without getting caught up emotionally in their predicaments that are offering them messages they need for their growth.

9. I act freely when I am tuned in, centered, and loving, but if possible I avoid acting when I am emotionally upset and depriving myself of the wisdom that flows from love and expanded consciousness.

DISCOVERING MY CONSCIOUS-AWARENESS

10. I am continually calming the restless scanning of my rational mind in order to perceive the finer energies that enable me to unitively merge with everything around me.

11. I am constantly aware of which of The Seven Centers of Consciousness I am using, and I feel my energy, perceptiveness, love and inner peace growing as I open all of the Centers of Consciousness.

12. I am perceiving everyone, including myself, as an awakening being who is here to claim his or her birthright to the higher consciousness planes of unconditional love and oneness.

THE SEVEN CENTERS
OF CONSCIOUSNESS

1. THE SECURITY CENTER.

This Center makes you preoccupied with food, shelter, or whatever you equate with your personal security. This programming forces your consciousness to be dominated by your continuous battle to get "enough" from the world in order to feel secure.

2. THE SENSATION CENTER.

This Center is concerned with finding happiness in life by providing yourself with more and better pleasurable sensations and activities. For many people, sex is the most appealing of all sensations. Other addictive sensations may include the sound of music, the taste of food, etc.

3. THE POWER CENTER.

When your consciousness is focused on this Center, you are concerned with dominating people and situations and increasing your prestige, wealth, and pride—in addition to thousands of more subtle forms of hierarchy, manipulation, and control.

4. THE LOVE CENTER.

At this Center you are transcending subject-object relationships and are learning to see the world with the feelings and harmonies of flowing acceptance. You see yourself in everyone—and everyone in yourself. You feel compassion for the suffering of those caught in the dramas of security, sensation, and power. You are beginning to love and accept everyone unconditionally—even yourself.

5. THE CORNUCOPIA CENTER.

When your consciousness is illuminated by this Center, you experience the friendliness of the world you are creating. You begin to realize that you've always lived in a perfect world. To the degree that you still have addictions, the perfection lies in giving you the experience you need to get free of your emotion-backed demands. As you reprogram your addictions, the perfection will be experienced as a continuous enjoyment of the here and now in your life. As you become more loving and accepting, the world becomes a "horn of plenty" that gives you more than you need to be happy.

6. THE CONSCIOUS-AWARENESS CENTER.

It is liberating to have a Center from which your Conscious-awareness watches your body and mind perform on the lower five centers. This is a meta-center from which you non-judgmentally witness the drama of your body and mind. From this Center of Centers, you learn to impartially observe your social roles and life games from a place that is free from fear and vulnerability.

7. THE COSMIC CONSCIOUSNESS CENTER.

When you live fully in the Sixth Center of Consciousness, you are ready to transcend self-awareness and become pure awareness. At this ultimate level, you are one with everything—you are love, peace, energy, beauty, wisdom, clarity, effectiveness, and oneness.

Reprinted from *The Handbook to Higher Consciousness* by Key Keyes, Jr., Fifth ed., copyright © 1975 by The Living Love Center.

Again, I wish to thank Ken Keyes, Jr., for permission to use material from his two life-enhancing books: *Handbook to Higher Consciousness* and *A Conscious Person's Guide to Relationships.* I strongly suggest you pick up copies of both at your favorite book dealer or write Living Love Publications for complete information on their courses, books, posters, cassette tapes and record albums.

Living Love Publications
790 Commercial Street
Coos Bay, OR 97420
(Ken Keyes and his staff moved from Kentucky to Oregon in the Fall of 1982.)

YOU NEED TLC

Human beings need Tender Loving Care. We thrive and grow on it. Without TLC, all kinds of negative emotional, mental and physical problems exist. We must learn to be tender (gentle) with ourselves. Most of us have made many mistakes in the past. Now, we have to forgive ourselves and let go of those past errors. We have nothing to feel guilty about. We were less aware then. Now we know better. By learning how to be tender and gentle with ourselves, we create the sensitivity to be tender in our dealings with others. To love your life is to learn to love all life.

Love is the answer. Love has unlimited power, including the power to heal and uplift every situation. When you learn to love yourself unconditionally, you will be able to love others without restrictions.

Take good care of yourself. You deserve the best of everything—love, health, riches, peace of mind—Total Success! Care enough for yourself to dare to believe you can have every good thing you desire. When you really care for yourself, you will be happy to share your riches—spiritual, mental and material—with others.

THE 3 Cs OF A LOVING RELATIONSHIP

I am indebted to a dear friend, Dottie Jirgal, for her beautiful definition of what makes a healthy relationship—"the 3 Cs of a loving relationship":

Communication
Commitment
Caring

On the Universal level, love is Communication at its highest form. It is Commitment to life itself, and it is Caring for all life.

On the personal level, Communication, Commitment and Caring are what make an intimate relationship between a man and a woman stimulating, strong and sensitive. The 3 Cs are also vital to a good relationship between parents and children and the bond that holds together all meaningful friendships.

UNIFICATION WITH ANOTHER

By using the power and intuition of Mind Science, we can actually experience the essence of another person through the process of unification. Inner Sensitivity allows this to happen. Although the gift of ESP (Extra-Sensory Perception) may play a part in this process, even ESP is secondary to the Knowingness that is within. In an intimate relationship, two individual minds come together in that inner space of the

One Mind. It is a beautiful, non-verbal communication tool used by more and more aware men and women.

When one continues to pray, meditate and study the teachings of the spiritual masters—Jesus, Buddha, Laotzu and other inspired spiritual leaders, plus absorb the writings of modern-day metaphysical teachers such as Ernest Holmes, Paramahansa Yogananda, Kahlil Gibran, Werner Erhardt, Ken Keyes, Jr., Jack Ensign Addington, Emmet Fox, Charles Fillmore, Richard Bach, Ann Meyer, Terry Cole-Whittaker and others—one realizes unification with another is not at all impossible. In reality, transcendental unification with All That Is is both possible and desirable.

All things are possible for the lover who is a believer. Love Unification with that woman or man you intend to share your life's experiences with can create the perfect dyad. Two beings coming together in spirit, mind, soul and body create a cosmic synergistic summit effect. The energy and power of two soul mates in unity with one another is awesome. When two become one, life acts upon life and love expresses itself at a climactic pinnacle. When two high conscious beings have sex, it becomes communication at its highest level. This is the creative spiritual mental and physical opportunity to love, be loved and become love. The result? Total love, total joy, total pleasure and total oneness. It is only in this unconditional manner that you can fully give of yourself and completely experience yourself and all of your beauty, love, good feelings and total magnificence.

SEX AND LOVE

When sex raises its lovely head, many people confuse

247

strong sexual urges with love. This reminds me of the modern cliche regarding sex: *IT AIN'T LOVE, BUT IT AIN'T BAD.* Like most cliches, this one rings basically true. Sex can be a beautiful experience. It can be the highest, most exciting form of communication between two people. It can be extremely pleasurable and life's number one turn on. It may be the best method to express the joy of love, although in and by itself it is not love. The two can be very compatible, but one can be present without the other.

Sexual stimulation presents a gratifying opportunity to love and be loved. Sex was not meant to offer a way to get anything. It is an exciting and fulfilling way to totally experience and enjoy yourself and another human being. In the blissful moment of ecstasy, at the zenith of orgasm, our earthly minds are stilled for a few seconds, and we experience oneness with everything.

At the point of climax, sex does unite with love itself. For a very brief period, our bodies, minds and emotions are overcome with pure joy. Since this cosmic love experience merges with sex for only a few orgastic seconds to intense sex partners, when experienced at all, sex alone is not the same as love. Love always heals and enhances everything it touches. Sex can pleasure and enhance us or it can be used by us or our partners as a manipulative device to "get something."

Sex at its best is exciting, intimate, loving communication, the giving and receiving of physical, mental and spiritual pleasure. Like all magnificent gifts, it can be misused and made destructive in the hands of the unaware.

Love is the absolute power of the universe. It alone cannot be perverted or misused. Our thinking can be positive or negative. Money can be manifested and sanctified by man's creative efforts or erroneously stolen by gunpoint. Sexual relationships can be joyful experiences or acts of aggression. Only love is omnipotent. Love is always positive, pure, powerful, joyous and life-enrichening. We may try to pervert it, but we cannot. To attempt to alter love is to simply see it disappear. It vanishes when we twist it, manipulate it or use it against ourselves or another. Love refuses to be used negatively. Love simply will disappear as soon as someone tries to misuse it. The misdirected person then may talk about love or try to convince himself or others that it is still there, but it won't be. Love, by its very nature, is unconditional and will not accept conditions and remain present in its truest form.

Love is never anything but good and always uplifts! Love never hurts; it always helps. However, lots of emotions that are not love often are mistakenly labeled as love, and many of these emotions do bring pain and suffering. Love only brings joy and happiness. When you're emotionally hurting and feeling sad or blue, something other than love is the reason.

The whole truth concerning life and love is found in the words of Dr. Ann Meyer, co-founder of the Teaching of the Inner Christ: **"LIFE IS CONSCIOUSNESS. CONSCIOUSNESS IS THE ONLY REALITY. LOVE IS THE ONLY POWER. JOY IS THE ONLY WAY."**

Sex, due to its very personalized nature, must be a very select expression of joy and good feelings. Love should be applied to all indiscriminately.

WHAT IS SEX?

Sex is about two bodies joyfully teasing and pleasing each other. It is physical communication that was intended to provide great pleasure to lovers. We do this beautiful act a great disservice when we approach it for any other reason than as an expression of love and/or intimate communication. Sex is not love, but it is the ultimate intimate gift lovers can give and receive.

The love we share with our parents or children may be unlimited in nature, and at the same time there are restrictions and taboos as to what lengths we can go to physicalize our expression of that deep love. When we come together with our mate or lover, there should be no limitations on our expression. Sex is the ultimate physical act. It is joyful unification with another for the purpose of experiencing joy.

Since sex is about physical pleasure, or should be, inviting your "reasoning" mind to bed with you and your partner is usually a big mistake. Your active mind generally will distract you from your pleasure. It is always overly concerned with what is happening, what does she/he think of me, am I doing it okay, will this get me the nonsexual thing I want from her/him, et. al.?

Sex is union. Sex can be a beautiful way to dissolve the illusion of separation. Unfortunately, our over-active "reasoning mind" can actually create the illusion of greater separation at the very moment we are united.

The only two perfect reasons to have sex with someone:

1. It makes you both feel good.
2. It is an expression of your intimate love.

While either of the above two reasons are singularly sufficient, the combination of both will raise the act to its most magnificent form.

Add any other considerations (money, outside favors, manipulation, etc.) and you greatly alter the expression of joy. There seems to be another reason for the sexual act that is entirely biological and usually one-sided—and this is for the sole purpose of intimacy and orgasmic release. This fact makes overt prostitution the world's oldest profession and keeps "business" flourishing today.

While this author believes in legalizing prostitution as a humane means of protecting women from racketeers and pimps who often use drugs and/or physical/psychological violence to maintain control over them, the best thing that can be said about prostitution is that we, as a society, have not yet transcended the need for it.

Too often sex is relegated to the status of a game. Emphasis on technique, frequency and endurance can turn the game into a contest, and the results may not be favorable. Keep it spontaneous and unrehearsed and the joy will naturally be greatly increased.

Thoughts concerning what "nice people" or "decent" women and men do in the privacy of the bedroom also inhibit free expression and unnecessarily add guilt to what was intended to be a joyous act.

Sex is an intimate physical act that can have deep emotion and spiritual meaning in the case of two soul mates coming together (the definition here for soul mate is: two people who find their highest personal expression of love—love for all things—when they spend time and space with each other) to share their magnificence. Sex can be an extension of true love. All human beings desire "closeness" and unity, even those who appear not to, and sex is intimate unification.

Your sexuality is a beautiful spiritual gift that you need never be ashamed of. It is a vivid and powerful part of you. It is connected to your very life force, and it is very good. Like any extremely powerful force, it should command your respect, and you can benefit by endeavoring only to use it for the joy and celebration of life, for which it was intended. To bastardize our creative sexual nature and misuse this sensuous power is to surrender our full right to life's most magnificent dance.

MEN AND WOMEN'S LIBERATION

The tail end of the twentieth century promises to be a time of great personal and planetary transformation. The Age of Aquarius is dawning and the New Age is being ushered in. Change is in the air and the old order is rapidly fading. Nowhere is change more evident than in the new definitions of male and female roles.

There is still some lingering conflict and nonsense on what it means to be a woman or man, but overall, both sexes are being accepted for what they really are—people!

We have discovered that women and men have far more in common than those few physical differences that puzzle interest and tantalize the opposite sex while seemingly making a statement about some apparent inherent differences. To believe that you can make a judgment on a person's nature by noticing her or his physical equipment is as foolish as supposing that all blondes have more fun than brunettes or redheads. Some blondes do and other blondes do not. We have been spoon-fed a bunch of stupidity on the subject of what it means to be a woman or man. The truth has always been that women and men are equal in every fundamental way. However, when nonsense is passed down from generation to generation, many people begin to buy into it and accept distortion as fact. This is exactly what has happened.

Men have only recently begun to realize that they are not inherently the gun-slinging, trail-blazing, super-aggressive never-say-die and never, never cry, stereotypes that they have been told they were. And women are rejecting the mindless fantasy that they are modern-day sisters to Cinderella, waiting for that handsome prince who will sweep them off their feet and take them to the never-never land of eternal happiness.

Some men still cling to their macho image. They won't allow themselves to feel and be sensitive. They don't know how to cry, but they are willing to die several years sooner than their female counterparts. Many women, too, will not give up the childish, romantic scenario still projected in many TV soap operas and Harlequin Romance novels. Their escape from reality may negate their opportunity to experience real happiness.

If women now seem to be making more progress than men in the areas of education, politics, business and professional careers, it is because their new liberation is more visible. While I salute women for the dramatic and long overdue changes their persistence is bringing about, I also feel the loving vibrations of the important, below-the-surface liberation both women and men are now experiencing. Total Success awaits all human beings who are willing to break the chains of self-imposed restrictions. Women's liberation also means men's liberation and visa-versa. Women and men are people, and all people were meant to be accepted, equal and free! Like everything tangible or intangible, true liberation begins in Mind and flourishes in an atmosphere of unconditional love.

FAMILY LIFE AND LOVE

Unconditional love pays noticeable dividends in the relationship between parent and child. The aware parent who loves without condition makes a valuable contribution to planetary transformation and New Age human enlightenment. Loving children without any conditions does not mean that you never discipline them; nor does it mean that they are not responsible for their behavior. What it does mean is that no matter what comes up, be it pleasing or disturbing to an adult, you never stop loving them, and you always let them know you love them, even when you do not approve of certain adolescent behavior. The loving parent may not always love the personality being expressed, but they always love the person. More importantly, they always clearly indicate to the child that he or she is loved and appreciated. The child develops self-esteem in this caring atmosphere of unconditional love. Higher love consciousness is obtained by

child and parent and the benefits of loving family relationships can bring joy, peace and harmony to a world that
threatens to explode due to the misguided thoughts and
deeds, symbolized by hate, war and international discord.

WHAT THE WORLD NEEDS NOW IS LOVE—
AND LOTS OF IT.

The closed, unsensitive family life conditions of certain
Middle East, male-dominated cultures represents a sobering
view of the havoc such suppression can bring. Children
lacking in self-esteem usually tend to perceive their world
as a hostile environment. Violence can become a way of life.
By practicing the principles of Total Success, a person can
overcome negative childhood conditions. Eventually all will
find the path that leads to love and enlightenment; however, without a lot of painful struggle, this can be realized by
those who receive the parental gift of constant love.

Frederick Perls, the world-renowned psychologist and
Gestalt therapist, offered this insight into thwarted child
upbringing and the break in emotions and conscious thinking: *"the split between conscious thinking and emotions
begins with a parent's conditional love."* Children who are
not rewarded for being themselves, who are always told they
can do better, find it very difficult to believe they are really
loved. An unloved infant or one who perceives he or she is
unloved, especially when under ten years old, is subjected to
a distorted impression of the world. Such a child will then
often strive to please or manipulate the parents through
various role-playing, in hopes of winning their love. The
result: A separation of conscious thoughts and inner feelings. To raise healthy children, we must (1) love our children

255

and (2) make certain they realize we love them.

All people love to be loved unconditionally. Children absolutely crave and thrive upon this pure expression of sharing and caring. Anna Westmoreland is a perfect example of a parent who reaped a love blessing by showering her five daughters with unconditional love. In her home, her love bond and personal respect was so powerful that she never experienced the trauma, discord and disrespect so many mothers and fathers experience when five children are all teenagers at the same time. Her relationship with her girls was (and is) always characterized by deep love, sharing, caring and respect. While many teenagers feel a need to rebel against their parents while in the process of leaving adolescence to become young adults, Anna's children felt no such desire to rebel against her. Instead, they continually return to her the love and affection she so unconditionally gave them.

Donna Diaz offers another shining example of the rich dividends that are the consequence of unconditional love. Working with young offenders and youth gangs within the ghettos of New York City, her generous out-pouring of unconditional love helped change dozens of hardened young lawbreakers into responsible members of society. "I hated some of their actions and deeds, but I always let them know I loved them," Donna told this author.

Donna became involved working with troubled youth when her own son began to use drugs and shoplift. She learned that he responded quickly to her experiment with unconditional love and changed direction in his life. "I would condemn his antisocial behavior and at the same time keep loving him." A strict Catholic, Donna believes unconditional love is God's answer to human problems. "The Lord hates sin," she is quick to point out, "but he loves sinners." Today her son is the vice-president of a bank in Boston, and many other young men and women are leading productive lives thanks to Donna Diaz's belief in the healing power of unconditional love.

We can learn much about the benefits of unconditional love from children. The more unconditional our love is for our children, the better they are equipped to meet life's challenges. To love a child unconditionally is to love life and its finest expression of itself. Children are only *ours* in the sense that we can assist them in their spiritual, emotional and physical growth. The beautiful, poetic words of *The Prophet* * by Kahlil Gibran speak this truth to us:

> *Your children are not your children,*
> *they are the sons and daughters of Life's longing for itself.*
> *They come through you but are not from you,*
> *And though they are with you, yet they belong not to you.*
>
> *You may give them your love but not your thoughts,*
> *for they have their own thoughts.*
> *You may house their bodies but not their souls . . .*

Love is the only true power. If we *own* it, we know freedom and have everything, for we never really own any other thing or person on the planet. We come into this world naked and without possessions, and we will leave it in the same way. Only love is eternal because love is what the Universe is about. Love, acting upon itself, gives birth to life.

To learn how to love is to learn the secret of the meaning

The Prophet by Kahlil Gibran, © 1923 & 1951. Published by Alfred A. Knopf, NY

of life. If you give love, you will receive love. By continuing to circulate love in your life, you will reach rare new heights of higher consciousness. Love is the reason for life itself.

We glorify all life by showering it with love. Love is the only power. All the nuclear bombs in the world cannot match the power of love. Bombs can only tear down, mutilate and kill living things. Love uplifts, makes whole and enhances all life.

Light your light and help others discover the love flame within them. Spread love from one end of the globe to the other. Do this and there will be no more hate or bombs or wars, or people who won't communicate with each other. Mental and physical disease will begin to disappear. Relationships will heal. Mankind will finally make peace with his environment.

Joy and peace are required to bring heaven to Earth, and love is the only way it can ever happen.

"True wonder is seeing the world without interpretation . . . "

—CARLOS CASTANEDA

"To be happy, see the light, be the light and then let your light shine . . . "

Chapter Eleven

HAPPINESS CAN BE YOURS

If you practice the principles set forth in this book, greater happiness will be yours. If you master nothing else but a loving nature and work on loving others unconditionally, you will be on the way to owning the whole world and everything in it.

Recently I became aware of still another insightful book by Ken Keyes, Jr. (I have already quoted liberally with permission, from his books, *A Conscious Person's Guide to Relationships* and *Handbook to Higher Consciousness* in Chapter Ten of this book). His latest book is titled, *Prescriptions for Happiness*. It presents, in Ken's easy, illuminating, down-to-earth style, three super prescriptions that can help anyone put more joy and aliveness into their lives.

Since I am in basic agreement with Ken's "happiness philosophy," and because Ken graciously wants to make his three *prescriptions* available to anyone on the planet who desires this knowledge, the following is his work, *Prescription for Happiness*, in its entirety. Read it with an open mind and reap the benefits!

To all my students
whose support
and dedication to their growth
helps me learn about
and pass on the
Science of Happiness—
and to all those
whose open and inquiring minds
will someday bring
these effective principles
into their lives.

I guess you know.

You've been shortchanging yourself.

You've been depriving yourself
of just about everything
that's really worth having in life—
ENERGY
INSIGHT
PERCEPTIVENESS
LOVE
PEACE OF MIND
JOY
WISDOM
AND A DEEP FEELING OF PURPOSE.

If it's any consolation,
most likely
everybody else you know
has been lousing up
his or her life,
too.

But you don't have to
keep on adding
to the dismal statistics
of unhappiness:

a life without much warmth and love,
worrying about money,
pushing yourself to do your job,
a turned-off marriage,
divorce, anxiety,
sexual restlessness,
boredom, loneliness,
fear, resentment, hatred,
frustration, anger, worry,
jealousy, irritation,
headaches, ulcers
and high blood pressure,
plus a general feeling
of queasiness and uneasiness
about everything
from your bank account
to the nuclear bomb.

Why
punish yourself
any longer?

You've been blaming
it all on others—
or on yourself.

But a part of you knows
it's only some
unskillful habit patterns
of your mind
that constantly set you up

for creating unhappiness
time after time!
Really look at
what you're doing
to yourself.

Is it possible
for you
to live a joyous
and happy life
with peace of mind
in our topsy-turvy world?

Yes Yes Yes Yes Yes Yes Yes
Yes Yes Yes Yes Yes Yes Yes Yes
Yes Yes Yes Yes Yes Yes Yes
Yes Yes Yes Yes Yes Yes Yes Yes
Yes Yes Yes Yes Yes Yes Yes Yes

IF—

This is a big IF.

Are you ready for it?

You can be happy
IF
you use the three
Prescriptions for Happiness
explained in this book.

These three prescriptions

really work.

They'll work
even if
you don't think
they'll work.

You may be telling yourself
that there is no way
they could work
in one of your life situations . . . .

But if you just take
these three prescriptions
and use them,
they will work for you
every time.

They're simple to understand.
They work—
if you do!

However, there is something
that will get in the way
of your applying them
in specific life situations
when you
most need them.

That something is you!
Actually
it's
not
really
you . . . .

It's only your mental habits,
and your selected memories
of how you think things are
that keep you from
molding things in your life
in a more harmonious way.

It's pride or
silly models of prestige
that get in your way.

Sometimes your mind would rather
prove itself right
than let you be happy!

But with practice,
you can learn
to handle these impediments.

I know you really want
to live a happy life.

We all do.

So let's get to work.

Here's the first
of the three
Prescriptions for Happiness:

KEN KEYES
Happiness Doctor

=====

℞

ASK FOR WHAT YOU WANT—
BUT DON'T DEMAND IT.

Use liberally as needed.
Memorize this prescription
so that you'll always have it
whenever you need it.

Refills: Anytime.

You stand a better chance
of getting what you want
when you ask for it
than when you don't.

That's obvious.

Why do you
often fail to ask
for what you want?
Sometimes you're afraid

that people
will be mad
at you
if you do.

Sometimes you hesitate
to assert yourself.

Perhaps you expect people
to read your mind.

Maybe you are practicing up
to become a martyr.

It's very simple—
just learn to ask
for what you want.

You don't have to pussyfoot
or play nicey-nicey.

You don't have to scream or yell.

You don't have
to fire up your mind
and make people
terribly wrong
if they don't do
what you ask.

You don't have to clam up.

You don't have
to retreat into
a deafening silence
that puts your relationship
into a deep freeze.

Just simply
ask for what you want—

without playing deceptive games,

without loading it down
with separating emotions
or implied threats,

without using
a heavy tone of voice.

Simply
but definitely
and specifically,
ask for
what you want!

Practice asking
for what you want
by noticing
how simply and directly
you can make requests
such as,
"Please pass the pepper,"
or
"Will you lock the door
when you leave?"

You'll be getting
the hang of it
when you can
ask for ANYTHING
in the same tone of voice
and with the same ease
as when you ask someone
to pass the pepper
or lock the door.

You will have to
practice a bit—
lots of bits!

You won't always find it easy
to ask for
money,
love,
sex,
or no sex,
assistance of various kinds
in a simple
yet specific
no-big-deal way.

Being simple,
direct and specific
without making
a pressure-cooker situation
out of asking
for what you want
is a skill
you will have to develop
if you want to live
a happier life.

Now let's look at
the second part of the prescription:
"but don't demand it."

A demanding act comes from
a demanding frame of mind.

Look at your separating feelings,
your attitudes and mental positions.

And then see how you

act out your demands:
by playing "poor me,"
by playing "you hurt me" and
by playing "if you really loved me . . . . "
and on and on.

This will take
a lot of practice
because we're all so used
to demanding
so many things.

Remember, you can demand
with a forceful tone
or with silent pursed lips.

It's your vibrations that count!

W hy do you
automatically demand
so much?

You're afraid people
won't treat you right
if you're not demanding.

You're afraid people
will run all over you.

So you make yourself very cactusy.

You're sure you're right—
and you want your rights
even if
you make yourself unhappy
getting your rights!

You feel that
when you spend
a lot of time with someone,

you'd better
shape up the person
so he or she
will fit your models!

But are you making
yourself happier
with all this demanding?

Do you really get
what you most want
in your life
through your demanding?

Are you really ready
to look
at how you are
addictively demanding
so many things of yourself,
of other people
and the world?

If you look closely
at the results you've had
from all the demanding
you've done recently,
I think you'll conclude
that even though
you're right,
the results you get
from demanding
are not all that good.

In other words,
most of the demanding you do

doesn't add
to your happiness.

You lose more happiness
than you gain.

You may discover
that a lot
of what you get
does not come
because of
your demanding it.

Why does it come?

It comes
because
it comes.

You're a part
of it all.

You have a right
to be here.

Sometimes you get
what you want
by demanding.

But it's like
losing a dollar
and gaining
a quarter!

When you either
loudly or softly demand
(instead of prefer)
you will lose:
insight,

humor,
enjoyment,
a feeling of love
(for yourself and others)
and your
peace of mind.

You've cheated yourself.

You never deserve
to be cheated by yourself.

How do you stop demanding?
It will mean loosening
the tight grip
YOU FEEL INSIDE YOU.

It will mean softening
the tones of your voice.

It will mean letting go
of that rock-like stance
you put on
when you ask for something.

It will mean that you
stop frowning
and feeling so serious
about the soap opera
we call life.

You'll probably
find it scary at first.
But with practice
it will be very relaxing
when you learn to ask for
what you want
without demanding.

It will mean taking the
this-is-such-a-heavy-problem tone
out of your requests—
along with all
the threatening
and worried
overtones.

It will mean sometimes
asking for things
with a ʋmile and a feeling of fun
showing that
you're tuned-in
to the way life
is just a cosmic joke
after all!

Non-demanding means
that you learn
to ask lightly—
often humorously.

It's like you're
playing the game
of trying to get
what you want—
but you're well aware
that you win some
and you lose some.

And it's O.K. to lose.

You can be a good sport
about the game of life.

Asking for what you want

without demanding
means that you stop hinting
about what you want.

It means that you don't put things
so obliquely that people will have to
try to figure out what you want.

It means you stop going around
with a heavy disposition
hoping someone will ask you
what's the matter.

It means you quit drowning yourself
by deciding in advance
that people won't want
to give it to you
or that you don't deserve
to get what you want.

It means that you learn
to ask again
for what you want TODAY—
even though you asked yesterday
without results.

Each day is
a new day.

You don't let
your memories of the past
hang over
and cloud up
the beautiful day
YOU CAN CREATE TODAY.

Now you're getting the hang

of Prescription No. 1:

"Ask for what you want—
but don't demand it."

That's the first of the three
Prescriptions for Happiness.

Here's the second
Prescription for Happiness:

KEN KEYES
Happiness Doctor

Rx.

ACCEPT WHATEVER HAPPENS—
FOR NOW.

Memorize this prescription
so that you'll always have it
whenever you need it.

Refills: Anytime.

This second prescription
may be the toughest one
for you to use.

"Accept whatever happens—for now"
may mean
that you'll have to learn
to accept the "unacceptable."

You may have
to forgive the "unforgivable."

You may have
to love the "unlovable."

You'll have to learn
to get your finger off
that emergency alarm button
in your mind
that keeps you wound up
so tight inside.

Do you really think
your survival is threatened
by the stuff
you're clinging to
or running away from?

It means that
you'll have to tell your mind
that what looks like
a catastrophe—
just ain't so!

There are many
other people
who are emotionally accepting
what you're making yourself
unhappy about.

If they can
accept the "unacceptable,"

perhaps you can, too.

Can you give yourself
the insight
that it's your struggle
and your demanding
that's making you unhappy?

It's not whatever
you're struggling over.

It's your emotion-backed demand,
not the life situation itself,
that causes your experience
of unhappiness!

Make a list of
all the things
you couldn't stand
last year—
and the year before.

Some of them
you've now learned
to emotionally accept.

This is called growth.

You're too wonderful
to keep yourself
from growing more.

Most of your life problems
can no longer
be effectively handled
by primitive
"fight or flight"

responses.

You usually deprive yourself
of getting the most
from the people and situations
around you
when you come on with power
or let your fears
make you run away.

To develop the most
satisfying outcomes,
most of your problems
require more insight and a
practical back-and-forth
working with the situation
over a period of time.

Try to remember
that it's always your
emotion-backed demands
that are really
the practical cause
of your own unhappiness.

The art of happiness
means learning to be with
and to work and play with
the cast of characters
you've brought into
your life.

Retreating won't do it.

Coming on
like a ten-ton truck
won't do it,

either.
Emotionally accepting
and patiently working
with life situations
will get you
the most that's gettable!

Remember that a lot
of human suffering
is caused by the mind
that takes offense
at what's happening.

You don't have to respond
to ANYTHING
by taking offense.
You can learn to forgive yourself—
and others.

Accepting may mean that
you look at what you do have—
and quit focusing so much
on what you don't have.

You constantly throw yourself
out of the experience
of enoughness
because your mind
is continuously preoccupied
with what you don't have.

You don't let yourself enjoy
what you have
here and now
in your life.

It's ridiculous
what you keep doing
to yourself.

You have so much—
but you take it
for granted.

You constantly
make your happiness
dependent on
what you don't have—
or getting rid of
something you do have!

Do you have
enough air to breathe,
enough food and water and
some shelter from the elements?

Everything else
you're emotionally demanding
(and losing happiness over)
is a neurotic game
your mind
is playing with you.

How long
are you going to let
your mind
destroy your happiness?

Whenever
you turn your mind loose,
hankering after
what you don't have,

you keep on creating
the experience of unhappiness.

Whenever you direct your mind
into noticing and appreciating
the beautiful things
you always have,
there's no end
to the happiness
you will experience.

It's your choice—
how you operate
your mind—
and your life.

Accept whatever happens—for now.

It doesn't mean you have to
like what's happening.

It doesn't mean you have to
stop trying to change
what's happening.

It doesn't mean you have to think
that whatever happens is right.

"Accept whatever happens—for now"
may mean:

You're going to stop
making yourself
so afraid, so angry,
so resentful, so worried—
and so unhappy.

You're going to prefer
that something be different—

but not addictively
demand it any longer!

You're going to change
your internal emotional experience.

Suppose you're mad at someone.

Do you hold on to your anger
because you believe
if you stopped being mad
it would make him or her
"right"?

Perhaps you need
more practice
in gently holding onto
what you feel is right
without creating anger
in yourself.

Do you hold onto
irritation and resentment
because you're embarrassed
to let go?

Look at all the uptightness
and tension
you're creating
in your body and mind.

Relax for your own sake.

You can enlarge your perspective.

You can let go of your negativity—
and your "me-vs.-you" resistance
even when you're right.

Does being upset
have to be
an unavoidable consequence
of being right?

When you're right,
you can be serene
and not lose
your peace of mind.

A skillful mind
can be right
in a given situation
and at the same time
let itself feel good
when people don't
agree with it.

To be happy
and feel good,
you can no longer afford
to let your mind
get away with criticalness
and disdainful judgmentalness
hiding under
a mask of politeness.

Let go of convincing others
that you're right—
and treat yourself
to happiness!

This accepting or letting go
is a sensitive
inner surrender—
not a forced
outer surrender.

INNER SURRENDER
is not based on
your feeling defeated.

It comes from

YOUR

OWN

INTELLIGENT

CHOICE.

It's based on INSIGHT—
not fear.

It's a wise decision
(even a purely selfish decision!)
that you make for yourself
to get more happiness
in your life.

It's a skill
you'll have to practice

It does not   .
come easily
to the human mind.

The letting go,
the inner surrender,
the non-demanding
we are talking about
IS VASTLY DIFFERENT
from defeat,
or submissiveness,
or a loss of strength,
or diminished effectiveness,
or loss of individuality.

Notice that
when you're defeated,
you don't really let go
of your inner demand.

You just turn loose
of the bone
you were fighting over.

You're still tormented inside
by an inner desire
that dominates
your consciousness—
you are still demanding the bone.

What we're talking about is
YOUR RELEASING YOURSELF
FROM INNER DESIRES
for what the world
is not ready
to give you
right here
and right now.

Wisely letting go
saves your energy,
clears your mind,
gives you sharper insights,
enables you to enjoy
the here-and-now moment
in your life
and helps you
increase your love
for yourself
and all other people.

As you learn
to emotionally accept it all,
you will heal the
THREE BLEEDING SEPARATENESSES
that keep you from getting
the most from your life.

You'll unify your psyche,
often divided against itself—
(your mind vs. your mind)
repressing, judging, downing you
and creating unpleasant feelings.

You'll heal the
mind-vs.-body split
that destroys your aliveness
by rejecting or ignoring your body,
its by-products or its desires—
and makes you feel half dead.

You'll no longer perpetuate
the me-vs.-others battle
that keeps you alienated from people
and destroys your joy of living.

This gentle letting go
of the demands
and attachments
of your mind
represents the highest level
of true strength
and character
in a human being.

Now let's look

at the last two words
in the second prescription.

What do we mean by
"for now"?

"For now" means "for now."
EVERYTHING IN LIFE CHANGES.

You'll be surprised
how often things
will change
and give you
what you want—
without your manipulating
or forcing them—
when you use the three
Prescriptions for Happiness.

"For now"
helps your mind
tune-in to
the here and now.

After all,
the here and now
is all
you've ever got.

You only have
the "now moment."

Yesterday is gathering dust
in the files of your brain.

And tomorrow is only a thought.

There will never be a tomorrow!

When tomorrow comes
it will always be "now."
That's why the
now moment
is "eternal"!

Don't give up
your now happiness,
thinking it will
all be better—
tomorrow.
It hasn't—
and it won't.
Now is it!
It's all you've got—ever.

Postponed happiness
may be
lost happiness.

So stop making yourself
so upset
because life is
the way it is.
In the precise here-and-now moment
there is nothing you can do
to change anything.
Maybe you can change it
one second from now—
or one month from now.
And it's O.K.
to play the game

of shaping things up
the way you want them.
JUST DON'T MAKE
YOURSELF UNHAPPY
IN THE MEANWHILE.

Why not be kind to yourself—
"for now"?
Relax your too active mind.
Our minds stay busy
regretting the dead past—
and creating concern
about the imaginary future.
NOW IS CONTINUALLY LOST!
Enjoy what's now—
even though
a part of it
is not the way
you want it to be.

One of the things
you haven't been willing to face
is that your life
will never meet
your mental models of perfection.
It's always been "imperfect."
It always will be "imperfect."
That's the way life is.

If you want to be happy
you'll learn to be with life

and accept life
the way it is—
which means
it will sometimes fit your expectations—
and sometimes it won't.

Sometimes life is lousy.

BUT YOU DON'T HAVE TO
MAKE YOURSELF FEEL LOUSY.

If your mind
will look around
it will see
that it always
HAS ENOUGH
to be happy!

If you'll just PREFER
that things be different,
you can enjoy your life.

And you can put energy
into changing
what you don't like.

But quit demanding
that they be different
from the way they are now—
even if you're right!

In other words,
the happy person
learns to live
with the daily "imperfections"
of his or her life.

As you grow

in awareness
you'll discover
that it's all perfect—
either for your growth
or your enjoyment!

Sometimes
you won't want
to grow so fast!

Sometimes you can use the past
for your present growth.

Look back again
over what's happened
in your life
during the past year . . . .

Did all your uptightness,
did all your fear, anger, jealousy,
worry, resentment, grief,
irritation and heartbreak
solve your problems?

Replay in your mind
the heavy dramatic "acts"
in the soap opera of your life
during the past year.

Can you see
how you could have used
the second prescription
"accept whatever happens—for now"
in every one of those situations
and you would not have had
to make yourself
so upset and unhappy?

Always remember
that the purpose
of the second prescription
is to try
to instantly stop
the way you've been
making yourself unhappy
time after time,
day after day.

These Prescriptions for Happiness
show you how to change
YOUR EXPERIENCE OF LIFE!!!
If you do this
you can let yourself
enjoy your life
all the time—
even when things go
from bad to worse.

As you increase your skill
in using the three
Prescriptions for Happiness,
you can be happy
most of the time.
To enjoy your life
most of the time,
you've got to realize
that the world
hasn't been doing it to you!

You've been doing it yourself!

The world rolls on—
and does what it does.

But only you can create
YOUR EXPERIENCE
of your life.

Now let's summarize
some of the things
your mind may forget·

You can emotionally
"accept whatever happens—for now"
and at the same time
you do not have to like
what happens.

You can try to change
whatever is wisely changeable
without setting up
more problems in your life.

To emotionally accept
whatever happens
means that
you don't even have
to give up your feelings
that what is happening
is wrong!

You just give up
making yourself unhappy!

You can create
an enjoyable experience
of your life—
even when things

aren't the way
you'd like them to be.

And that begins to happen
when you learn to
"accept whatever happens—for now."

As long as you live,
you'll win some
and you'll lose some.

Your life
will sometimes seem "perfect"
and sometimes seem "imperfect."

Things will go up and down.
BUT YOUR EXPERIENCE OF LIFE
DOES NOT HAVE TO GO
UP AND DOWN!!!

Good luck.
Remember, you can
master your mind
when the going gets rough.

You're now ready
for the third
Prescription for Happiness:

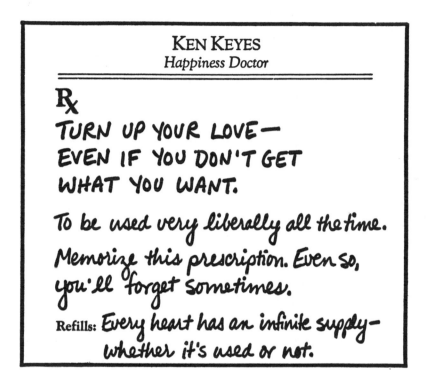

KEN KEYES
Happiness Doctor

℞

TURN UP YOUR LOVE —
EVEN IF YOU DON'T GET
WHAT YOU WANT.

To be used very liberally all the time.
Memorize this prescription. Even so,
you'll forget sometimes.

Refills: Every heart has an infinite supply —
whether it's used or not.

I'll bet you think
that the third
Prescription for Happiness
suggests that you
"turn up your love"
in order to be nice
to other people.
That's not it.

**YOU TURN UP YOUR LOVE
TO BE NICE TO YOURSELF!**

Can you see
that you've been making yourself
separate and unhappy
because you've kept
your love turned off—
toward yourself
and other people?

What do we mean by love?

Love isn't kind acts
or gifts wrapped
with a bow on top—
although love may lead you
to do these things.

Love means
tearing down the separateness
and the boundaries
between your heart feelings
and another person.

Love is just
a feeling
of togetherness
and openness
in your heart.

Actually,
when you love someone
it means that
he or she
is putting you in touch

with a part of you
that you love
in yourself.

Conversely,
notice that when
you're rejecting someone,
he or she
is only doing
what you would strongly reject
in yourself!
The world is your mirror . . . .

Love is a feeling of closeness,
of warmth,
of nonseparateness,
of understanding,
of togetherness—
of oneness.
Love is not a matter
of what happens in life.
It's a matter of
what's happening
in your heart.

Most people
aren't very skillful
in loving.
They create difficulties
in loving themselves
and other people.

They think
that if they love someone,
they've got to like everything
the person says and does.

They think it means
they're obligated
to do something.

They think love means
you can't say "no"
to someone you love.

As a skillful lover
you can tell yourself
(and even others),

"Whether I like
what you do or say
has no effect on
whether I love you
or not.

"I don't have to love
your actions—

"IT'S YOU I LOVE."

To whatever degree
you have strings
attached to your love,
you're not really loving.

In other words
the game is to
"love everyone unconditionally—
including yourself."

Always remember,

love is a heart feeling—
it is not what you say or do
although your feeling of love
will definitely
have an influence
on many of your actions.

When you get right down to it—

**You love a person
because he or she
is there.
This is the only reason.**

You don't love people
because they desperately
want your love.

You don't love people
because they need it.

You don't love people
because they deserve it.

You don't love people
because you want them
to love you.

(Some may not
allow themselves
to love you.)

You just love them—
because they're there!

Notice that love doesn't work
as a barter or an exchange.

"I'll love you if you love me"
is usually ineffective.

Here's what works perfectly
to increase your happiness:

"I'll love you no matter
what you say or do.

"I'll love you always.

"No strings.

"No barter.

"No exchange.

"No bookkeeping.

"My love just is—
because we are here."

"I may not want
to be with you sometimes
because I don't like
the roles
that you play
in the soap opera
of life.

"But I'll always love you.

"I'll always
have that
heart-to-heart feeling
that I create in me
when I think
of you."

How do you increase
your feeling of love for people?

Hug them more often or
look into their eyes more deeply
to help you open up and experience
the human being that is there—
that is just trying,
skillfully or unskillfully,
to get his or her life
to work better.

Share with others
your most secret thoughts.

Experience everything
that everyone does or says
as though you had done or said it.

Help them in caring ways.

To love more deeply,
open your eyes to see and appreciate
the beauty that is in your own life.

Become more aware
(perhaps by making lists)
of the things that are lovable
about you and your world.

This will lead you automatically
into experiencing the beauty
and lovableness
of the people around you.

As you open your heart,
perhaps slowly at first,
you will soon discover
that people respond
by opening their hearts to you.

Before you know it

your love will be increasing
not as a word
or as another "should,"
but as a vital feeling
you create in your heart.

To increase your love
imagine that someone's heart
is inside your heart
and that both hearts
resonate together.

Put yourself in his or her shoes
so that you can understand—
with both your mind
and your heart.

Understanding
with your heart
gives you emotional contact
with another person.

Understanding
with your mind
means to honor and accept
the value of the lessons
life is offering
the other person.

Wisdom
is the compassionate blend
of both the
heart and mind.

Now let's look

at the second part
of the third prescription,
which says
to turn up your love
"even if you don't get what you want."

You don't need this prescription
to turn up your love
when you get what you want.

It's easy to love
when the sun is shining
and you're getting your way!

You don't need this book
to tell you how to be happy then.

To be a skillful lover
you must be able
to keep your own heart open
to another person
no matter what's happening
in the soap opera
of your life.

You can throw someone
out of your melodrama.
BUT DON'T THROW HIM OR HER
OUT OF YOUR HEART!

What you've got to learn
if you want to create
a happy life
is to
turn up your love
even when you're not

getting your way! ★ !#!

You'll have to practice this.
It doesn't come easily—
except with dogs.

Have you ever noticed
how often a dog
will wag its tail
and keep on loving you—
even if you don't
take it everywhere you go
or feed it on time?

A dog doesn't withhold love
to control you.

If you can train yourself
to make your love
as unconditional
as that of most dogs,
you'll have it made!

You really know this.
You just keep forgetting it.
Christ said, "Love one another."

Love is a central theme
in every religion.

Our lives are set up
to give us a head start
with a big dose
of unconditional mother-love
when we first
come into the world.

Your life
can be successful,
wealthy,
prestigious
and influential.

But it won't be enough.

You will not reach
your potential for happiness
unless you experience
a lot of love
for yourself and
for other human beings.

Love is more powerful
than all
the bombs on earth
put together.

Love can bring peace—
bombs will not.

People will do things freely
from the love in their hearts
that they would never do
without their love
no matter how much
you bribe
or threaten them.

All human beings
are either near
or distant relatives
to each other.

Our human-to-human love

that experiences all people
as "US"
is the only possible way
to bring peace,
harmony,
cooperativeness
and enjoyment of life
to the four billion people
on this earth.

We couldn't fight wars,
either personal
or international,
if we had
more love
in our hearts.

It's easy to love
those who love you.

But are you skillful enough
to keep your love
turned up in your heart
even when you think
that other people are
hating you,
ridiculing you,
downing you,
refusing to be with you
or are doing things
to hurt you?

If you develop a high level of skill
in keeping your love turned up
(even when you don't get what you want)

you can elect yourself
a member of
the lovers' club!

Don't worry about whether
other people are loving you.

That's their problem.

As you increase your skill
in living a happy life,
your ONLY concern
will be whether YOU are
loving other people.

You can learn to put your love
on automatic
regardless of whether
they reflect back
your love.

You can always create
your own experience of life
in a beautiful and enjoyable way
if you keep your love
turned on within you—
regardless of what
other people say or do.

So let's go beyond ourselves.

We can learn
to turn up our love—
even when we don't
get what we want.

We can extricate ourselves
from the clashing

separate identities
we are so valiantly defending.

We can free ourselves
from who we think we are
so that the beautiful beings
we are deep inside
can come out and play
with the other beautiful beings
around us.

We've got to convince
our egos
and our minds
that if we want
to live happy lives,

**love
is
more
important
than
anything
else!**

So now you've got
all three
Prescriptions for Happiness:

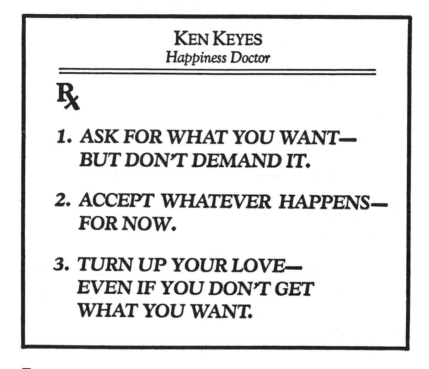

KEN KEYES
Happiness Doctor

℞

*1. ASK FOR WHAT YOU WANT—
BUT DON'T DEMAND IT.*

*2. ACCEPT WHATEVER HAPPENS—
FOR NOW.*

*3. TURN UP YOUR LOVE—
EVEN IF YOU DON'T GET
WHAT YOU WANT.*

It takes skill and insight
to use these
Prescriptions for Happiness.

They're not as easy
as taking a pill.

You have to work with
your desire systems,
your ego,
your selective memory,
your mental habits

311

and your illusions
of your pride and prestige.

For the rest of your life
you'll need to work on yourself
using these prescriptions.

But it's a lot easier
than all the misery
and unhappiness
you put yourself
through
when you ignore these
Prescriptions for Happiness.

It may take you months
or even years
to acquire the skill
to use these guidelines.

You've got to learn
to use them
in your heavier life situations—
which is the time when
you need them most.

So try not to let yourself
get discouraged—
and for your happiness' sake,
don't ever give up!

You probably
won't ever be able
to apply these prescriptions
perfectly.

You're not addicted
to always meeting your models,

are you?!?

You don't have to apply them perfectly.
The more you apply them,
the more you get the benefits.
Be content with more or less,
rather than all or none.

So now you've got it.

There's only one person
in the world
that can really
make you happy.
There is only one person
in the world
that can really
make you unhappy.
How about
getting to know
this person
more deeply?
For starters,
go look
in the mirror
and smile
and say,
"Hello."

And then tell yourself
that for a while
you're going to quit

putting so much energy
into trying to change
the people around you.

It hasn't worked
that well,
has it?

Instead,
you're going to put your energy
into doing the inner work
on your own mind
that will enable you
to use these
Prescriptions for Happiness
skillfully and effectively
in your daily life.

Life goes by rapidly.

Don't delay.

Don't put it off.

Don't wait until
you have some
spare time.

Don't wait until
the time's "right."

Don't let the mind
that you're trying to retrain
talk you out of doing it!

Your mind's
really good at this.

Your mind will come up

with lots of reasons
for not following
the three prescriptions.

Keep telling your mind
that you are determined
to do it!
Tell your mind
you want to live
a life characterized by:
ENERGY,
INSIGHT,
PERCEPTIVENESS,
LOVE,
PEACE OF MIND,
JOY,
WISDOM,
AND A FEELING OF PURPOSE.
Ask your mind to help you.
It's your friend, you know.
And if you're determined,
it will give you
what you want.

Do you really want
to use the prescriptions
or do you
just want to want
to do it?
Don't wait any longer

for the people around you
to make you happy.

Don't wait for the world
to fit your models
closely enough
so you can create
the experience
of peace and enjoyment.

HAPPINESS IS A DO-IT-YOURSELF
GAME!

AND TIME IS PASSING!

Loving more and demanding less

are not only
the nicest things
you can do
for yourself.

They're also
the most caring things
you can do
for the whole world!

These three prescriptions
are actually quite contagious.

The more you use them yourself,
the more the people around you
will use them—
even if you don't tell them
about the prescriptions.

They'll just pick them up.

And the children around you
will learn to use them
as automatically
as they absorb a language.

But here's
a word of caution:

Don't demand
that others use
these prescriptions.

Such demands
(even though you're right!)
will only
decrease your happiness.

Let them learn
BY YOUR EXAMPLE—
and not by
your preaching.

It can't be taught.

It has to be caught!

The effect of using the
Prescriptions for Happiness
will seem like
a miracle to you—
and perhaps to others.

Actually, miracles
are normal everyday events
for people who skillfully use
these principles
moment by moment
in their lives.

After all,
a miracle is something
you would like to have happen
that you didn't expect.

The results
in your life
that you will get
by using the
Prescriptions for Happiness
may seem
like miracles to you
because you've never tuned-in
to the real power of love.

Love helps things
get rearranged,
harmonized and settled
without our bruising
or harming each other.

Be sure to memorize the
Prescriptions for Happiness
so they'll be right there
when you need them:

1. Ask for what you want—
   but don't demand it.

2. Accept whatever happens—for now.

3. Turn up your love—
   even if you don't get what you want.

Don't let life
catch you
without these prescriptions.

They'll help you create
the happiest life
you can possibly have.

And remember,
you're always
beautiful,
capable and
lovable
even if you don't
always succeed
in using the three
Prescriptions for Happiness.

I love you,

Continuing Your Growth

If you want some help,
there's a lot of it available.

To begin with,
keep rereading this book.

It's all in here,
although you may not understand
how wonderfully it works
to unravel the knots
in your life
when you first read it.

Cornucopia is a college
that offers courses

from a weekend to a month
that give you actual practice
in creating a happy life
in everyday living situations—
in your marriage,
in your business
and in all areas
of your life.

Cornucopia
also offers
weekend workshops
in most of the larger cities
in the nation
from time to time.

By sending for a catalog
you can be tuned-in
to these workshops
that are happening
within a few minutes
or a few hours
from where you live.

To get more information
or a free catalog
you can
write or phone:

Cornucopia
790 Commercial Street
Coos Bay, OR 97420

Reprinted from *Prescriptions to Happiness* by Ken Keyes Jr.,
Living Love Publications

These books by Ken Keyes, Jr., will help you increase your skill in creating a happier life—

A Conscious Person's Guide to Relationships, by Ken Keyes, Jr.
$3.95. This guide shows you how to use the techniques of Living
Love to create a more delightful relationship with the person you
have chosen to live with. Seven guidelines are offered for entering into a relationship. There are also seven guidelines for being
in a relationship, and seven guidelines for decreasing your involvement in a relationship. It is enjoyable to read, realistic in its
approach and immensely helpful if you have a relationship or
wish to find one. It will show you how to gradually create the
high level of love and enjoyment you've wanted to share with
the person you live with.

Handbook to Higher Consciousness, by Ken Keyes, Jr. $2.95.
This is the basic text in the Living Love system. It introduces five
Methods and the Consciousness Doubler for working on your
addictive demands. It has chapters on applying these life-giving
principles to different areas of your life. Countless people have
experienced that their lives have changed dramatically from the
time they began to use the practical methods explained in the
Handbook to Higher Consciousness.

How to Make Your Life Work or Why Aren't You Happy? by
Ken Keyes, Jr. and Tolly, $2.00. In this delightful introductory
book, every other page is a cartoon. It is ideal as a gift for
people you want to introduce to this helpful approach to
expanding their lives.

Taming Your Mind, by Ken Keyes, Jr. $5.95 clothbound.
This is an effective guide to making sound decisions. The helpful
"tools for thinking" are illustrated by 80 drawings by Ted Key.

These books are available through bookstores or by mail from
Living Love Publications. Please enclose 75¢ per book for post-
age and packaging. Kentucky residents add 5% for sales tax.

For information on other books, trainings, cassettes and posters, or to have your name placed on the mailing list, you may
write to:

LIVING LOVE PUBLICATIONS
790 Commercial St., Coos Bay, OR 97420

I'm very grateful to Ken Keyes, Jr. His wise insights helped me get through my "Love" chapter, and permission to reprint his beautiful little book, *Prescriptions for Happiness,* made this chapter a snap! Love and Happiness are HEAVY DUTY subjects. I have not always expressed my real love. When I am totally one with unconditional love, I am in a happy state of being. When I'm not completely happy, I notice I am not expressing my love.

Love and happiness are the divine, dynamic duo. When I'm with them, I am beautiful, powerful and filled with joy. So will you be when you totally experience love in your life.

Love brings happiness and happiness always embraces love. Together, they are what life is all about. I want all the love and happiness possible in my life! How about you?

The only way to experience love and happiness, is to **be** *love and be happy.*

*"By the way, what are you doing
to become a hero? Don't blush
at your greatness, actualize it!"*
—ALFRED KORZYBSKI

"Having more of life
and less of death
is what it's all about . . . "
—JAMES BUGENTAL